William Bender Wilson

A few acts and actors in the tragedy of the Civil War in the United States

William Bender Wilson

A few acts and actors in the tragedy of the Civil War in the United States

ISBN/EAN: 9783337220556

Printed in Europe, USA, Canada, Australia, Japan

Cover: Foto ©ninafisch / pixelio.de

More available books at **www.hansebooks.com**

CONTENTS.

	PAGE.	PAGE.
DEDICATION,		5
JOHN BROWN,	7 to	14
IMPERIALISM THE MOTIVE FOR SECESSION,	15 to	21
PREPARATIONS FOR WAR—THE FIRST TROOPS TO RESPOND,	22 to	30
CURTIN AND ANDREWS,	30 to	31
"HONOR TO WHOM HONOR IS DUE,"		32
THE COCKEYSVILLE CAMPAIGN AND FITZ JOHN PORTER,	33 to	41
FITZ JOHN PORTER,	41 to	45
BULL RUN TO ANTIETAM,	46 to	72
THE AMMUNITION TRAIN,	72 to	82
A TRIP FROM FREDERICK CITY TO CHAMBERSBURG, AND A VIEW OF THE LATTER'S DESOLATION,	83 to	89
THE RAILROAD IN WAR TIMES,	90 to	95
U. S. MILITARY TELEGRAPH CORPS,	96 to	102
ABRAHAM LINCOLN,	103 to	114

TO MY WIFE AND CHILDREN:

There are periods which come to all when the noise of the world's activities seems to cease for a moment to allow us the time to turn our thoughts inward for the purpose of reviewing life with its hopes, its failures and its possibilities.

Such reviews must necessarily place on the tablets of memory many pictures taken from the world's ever-moving panorama, which by producing in words, or on canvas, may be profitable to our kind.

One of these periods recently came to me, and the review covered in point of time five-sevenths of the allotted years of man, for when the bells in the birth-day tower next chime for me I will have completed the cycle of a half of a century of life existence with its varied experiences and recollections.

I have taken a number of pictures from memory's tablets as they came up in the review and now grouping them together under the title of "A Few Acts and Actors in the Tragedy of the Civil War in the United States," lovingly dedicate their publication to you.

WILLIAM BENDER WILSON.

"WALDON," HOLMESBURG,
    Philadelphia.

NOTES ON THE CIVIL WAR.

I.

JOHN BROWN.

JOHN BROWN'S acts at Harper's Ferry constituted the hand-writing on the national wall which warned the world of the coming of that great struggle of which those acts were but a forerunner.

In the light of constitutional government and its preservation, the movement upon Harper's Ferry can only be viewed with condemnation, for it was a movement wherein liberty degenerated into license and lawlessness. There was, however, something bordering upon the sublime in the bearing and motives of the prompter and chief actor in the movement that must command the admiration of all fair-minded people, and it is from this point of view that this sketch is drawn: Condemnation for the methods pursued—recognition of the bearing and motives of the man.

It was on a bright June day in 1859, whilst standing at the railroad station in Harrisburg, I saw John Brown as he stepped on board a train on the Cumberland Valley Railroad preparatory to his going to Harper's Ferry and his fate. I had seen him before, but I little dreamed, as I looked upon him that day that he was taking a step that was only the initiative to a tremendous fraternal strife so soon to follow, or that as he crossed the Susquehanna he would never return, or that his ebb would be a stream of blood reaching to the banks of that river.

John Brown sprung from the humblest walks of life, passed through scenes of bloodshed, attracted the eye and commanded the attention of the world.

There was an air of nobleness and dignity about his person. He was grand and majestic in proclaiming what he esteemed the truth, and strong and mighty in the execution of its behests. As free as the air of his native Connecticut, he was outspoken in according the same freedom to others and dauntless in aiding them to maintain it.

The terrible curse of slavery was on this country. The Christian Church, mistaking its mission, either openly advocated slavery, or by its silence consented to it; the Government sustained and supported it, statesmen coquetted with it, while the populace were more than prepared to denounce, or, if their passions were aroused, to mete out violence to the man or men who would dare to intimate its abolition. Knowing this, yet believing in the divine right of all persons to enjoy personal liberty under the restraints of Divine law only, John Brown did not hesitate to pronounce in favor of the abolition of slavery. He believed that the Americans, the mightiest as well as the wisest of people, should rise to the height of the duties of the hour and decide the question upon the grounds of consistent justice. That America's mission was not simply to elevate the liberties of those colorless people who were so fortunate as to dwell within her borders, but that she had the higher, nobler one of obliterating the color line and of giving to the inhabitants of the Universe a system of government whose sole basis should be the consent of the governed.

He recognized what an element of strength to the enemies of popular government was the cry of American inconsistency, as well as the fact that that inconsistency could not be disproved so long as we held up our idea as one of equality of all men, and at the same time practiced the binding on of shackles to men, women and children.

Believing this, John Brown was not one to hide himself behind high-sounding theories of government and shirk the duties that one man owes to another.

He sought not personal advancement by the means of political parties. He could have thrown his commanding talents into the arena of partisan politics, and possibly, probably, have become eminent as a politician; but personal advancement had no attractions for him.

He aimed to be right—not popular; to advance his fellow man—not himself.

He knew that any of the then existing means of convincing men of error and of bringing them up to the duty line from his standpoint would fail. That to convince them, or to bring them up to that line, would require some bold, prompt action that would startle and astound the world and place thought upon the scent of right. With this in view he made his movement upon Harper's Ferry.

He comprehended that the movement was a direct violation of the written law of the land; that its failure would bring upon himself the loss of life and entail upon his fame and family the spot that death upon the gallows leaves. But it did not deter him.

He moved on, captured Harper's Ferry, and demanded, not gradual emancipation, not emancipation by compensation, not emancipation as a political necessity, but the immediate and absolute abolition of slavery because slavery was wrong.

He was not wrong in his conclusions as to the effect that would follow such a bold and prompt action. It did startle and astound the people; it did release thought from the shackles of policy which had bound it. Agitation became the order of the hour, and continued until the last bond was stricken from the last bondsman.

For his movement upon Harper's Ferry John Brown was termed crazy by that conservative element who, not desiring to place themselves in the position of approving slavery, yet disapproved of any action that was offensive to the keen sensibilities of the slaveholder. There is not a single fact upon which to base an assumption of insanity. It is a common thing to raise the cry of insanity as the most convenient way out of the acceptance of an unpleasant truth.

But where in the world has the man arisen who, grasping at a great truth which had either remained unseen, unknown or unacknowledged by the masses, and having had the boldness, the fearlessness to proclaim it, has not been greeted with similar words of denunciation? The world of letters, of science, of invention, of politics, of religion, is full of instances where the greatness of man in its dawn emits a dazzling light that dulls the perceptions of those upon whom it falls, bringing from them condemnation and derision.

When the Heavenly-inspired Paul, turning aside from the attractions of place and power, accepted a great though unpopular truth, boldly and fearlessly proclaimed it, he was called a madman.

When Paul delivered that speech of matchless eloquence, proclaiming the freedom of all through Christ, that caused King Agrippa to forget that he was an anti-Christian Jew and wrung from his manhood the confession, "Paul, almost thou persuadest me to be a Christian," Festus, the Roman Governor who was present, exclaimed with a loud voice, "Paul, thou art beside thyself, much learning doth make thee mad." The world of Festus believed that Paul was mad and took up the cry. But who believes it to-day? Does any one?

It may be said this comparison should not be drawn.

Why not? Paul was battling for the freedom of the soul of man—was aiming at releasing it from the shackles that bound it to the devil. John Brown was battling for the freedom of the person of man and aimed at breaking the shackles that bound his hands and feet and wounded the soul.

John Brown at Harper's Ferry announced his

government and proclaimed his purpose. He maintained his position for days against great odds before he was taken prisoner. His trial and execution followed. The failure to immediately reap the fruits of his movement was owing to the fact that those who were to be benefited by it, through ignorance, did not comprehend his plans. But that his movement was not a failure is patent to the thinker of to-day.

It was the knell that sounded slavery's doom.

John Brown issued the edict at Harper's Ferry that the slave should be free, and General Grant proclaimed to the world from Appomattox that the freedom of the slave was an accomplished fact.

Brown at Harper's Ferry and Grant at Appomattax were logically cause and effect.

What John Brown had done was heralded to the world. It fell upon the bondman as a great light, inspiring him with hope, strength and courage, awakened him to his duties to himself, and when the irrepressible conflict which John Brown had inaugurated burst out in all its fury he was found intrenched in the right.

I say this without reservation. For the loyal mass of the disloyal region, who, surrounded by the power of educated traitors, remained steadfast to the Government, were those of the darkened skin. Although their minds were untutored and darkened by the heavy clouds of slavery, yet they were by intuition intensely loyal.

Rarely in the history of the rebellion has there been an instance recorded where a slave voluntarily raised his hand against the Government. On the contrary, every page is marked with the fact that he was the white man's equal in devotion to the cause they were fighting for, and side by side with the white man he laid his life upon the altar of freedom, a willing sacrifice to that devotion.

The testimony of all our leading military men will bear me out in saying that by their wonderful intuitive system of inter-communication in the insurgent States, used solely for the benefit of the Government, the slaves gave an aid to military operations whose value can hardly be estimated. And soldiers who after suffering untold horrors in Southern prisons made their escape attribute their success in so doing to the slaves' assistance.

John Brown's soul was marching on.

What John Brown did was done from his own volition at the dictation of duty impelled by a sense of right. He was to be admired in his humanity, but to be condemned in his citizenship. He was a good man, but he over-rode law and suffered the penalty.

II.

IMPERIALISM THE MOTIVE FOR SECESSION.

SO MUCH has been written on the causes leading up to the stupendous strife that robbed this wonderful country of streams of precious blood which flowed continuously for four long weary and dreary years, that I crave pardon for dwelling a moment upon them as they were presented to my mind at the time.

In the spring of 1860, having just attained my majority, I undertook a journey through the Southern States for the purpose of informing myself of the practical results of slavery, and of obtaining a consensus of opinion upon what the people of those States wanted in the form of government and what they expected from the then existing form.

I found the public mind very much excited and inflamed by the passage of personal liberty bills and emigration laws by some of the Northern States, by the acts of John Brown at Harper's Ferry, and by the aggressive attitude of the Republican party in the campaign it was then making precedent to the Presidential election fast approaching.

The mass of the people with whom I came in contact believed that the people of the North intended making violent encroachments upon the rights, privileges and institutions of the South and were preparing, where not ready, to resent them.

The leaders, however, of public sentiment, the able and cultivated men who ruled by force of intellect, wanted revolution. To attain their desire they cultivated the passions of the people by coloring and exaggerating the foolish harangues of Northern fanatics and the unfriendly enactments of Northern legislatures. The Republic, as a democracy, they despised and in consequence were ever in readiness to conspire to change its form of government into a National aristocracy.

Nature had been lavish of her gifts to the semitropical States whose shore lines were washed by the waters of the Gulf of Mexico. The territory covered by them seemed to these leaders to be peculiarly adapted for the foundation of an Empire, while to the south and west, just beyond the Rio Grande, stretching from the Gulf of Mexico to the Pacific Ocean, lay the land of the Aztecs.

Mexico—a country one of the fairest on the face

Imperialism the Motive for Secession.

of the earth, with a soil unexcelled in fertility, a climate unequalled in its varied gradations; a country abounding in mineral wealth and precious stones, with capabilities for an extended commerce and for agricultural development, and one whose people had no settled opinions of what should constitute stable government, presented a dazzling picture for Imperial acquisition and extension. It was a bright dream and ever present to the minds of the leaders. It is, therefore, not astonishing that they astutely turned every argument that presented itself against the Government of the United States and towards educating the Southern masses to revolt. Imperialism was the hidden basis of all political action, and unwise utterances and unwise legislation in the North gave to its devotees the opportunity of presenting to the people fallacious arguments which should tend towards establishing it as a form of government on this continent.

It was my privilege to come in contact with some of the leaders and, although they were professedly favorable to a Republic, I could see beneath their republican garb the colors of royal robes protruding.

While stopping at the Assembly House in Columbia, South Carolina, on the eve of the Secession Convention meeting in that city, I met Robert Barnwell

Rhett, a man of brilliant attainments, an inveterate hater of the American Union, and one who enjoyed being looked upon as the first man in Congress to propose a dissolution of that Union. Mr. Rhett had just emerged from his self-imposed retiracy to private life, in which he had waitingly lingered for a decade of years to take the helm and steer his State on the stormy sea of revolution. During an evening spent in the parlor a number of gentlemen were discussing the political situation—it was after Mr. Lincoln's election. One cautious gentleman argued that South Carolina had no tangible cause to secede; that the burning questions of the hour were mere abstractions so far as it was concerned; that the State would not lose one slave by the unfriendly operations of the personal liberty bills; that the people were not nomadic in character, and not one would be affected by the unfriendly operation of laws to govern the Territories; that Mr. Lincoln's administration, no matter how much it might desire to do so, could not injure the State, for the reason that the co-ordinate branches of the Government, the judicial and legislative, as then constituted in their personnel, were a barrier to any encroachments by the Executive. Mr. Rhett, who had been a respectful and attentive listener, cut the argument off by admitting its force and frankly saying that it was revolution of the government that was wanted and that revolution would be had. A few days thereafter, under the leadership of Mr. Rhett, the ordinance of secession was passed at Charleston, the first scene in the opening act of the great tragedy which had been carefully plotted for presentation to the American people.

In the preceding summer I had been stationed in Montgomery, Alabama, and while there I saw William Lowndes Yancey taking the platform as he started on his campaign of firing the Southern heart, which was to lead him and his section to their fate.

Mr. Yancey was a South Carolinian by birth, and a true outcome of that aristocratic portion of the people of the South who believed in the Divine right of kings to rule, or, in the absence of kings, that the land owner had the same kind of right to absolute control of all that might be necessary to the cultivation of the land, whether men or cattle. He was earnest and honest in his advocacy of his views, and in consequence it was to be expected that he would be found on the side of the few and against the many. He was the most brilliant of that coterie wherein Ruffin, Rhett and Keitt were shining lights and which truthfully represented the class that was infatuated by the dream of Empire.

As the class thought it saw in the Gulf States the rising of the Empire so did Mr. Yancey, and he gave all of his great abilities, his remarkable eloquence, his untiring energy and his exclusive time to bring about the realization of the dream.

His personal appearance was faultless; his speech pure, smooth and magnetic. There was not an impurity in his public or private character. It was, therefore, expected as he moved along on his mission, he would be able to bring not only devotees to the altar, but converts too—an expectation which was fully realized.

Fiery and impetuous in the extreme South, he modified his language as he moved northward, because he knew that the stimulus for precipitating the Gulf States into revolution would not answer in the border States. The effect of his diplomacy was the drawing of most of the border States into the secession movement—a movement that was expected to be only preliminary to the total revolution of the form of government in the Gulf States. He aided in the formation of the Southern Confederacy, which he looked upon solely as being the halting ground between the Republic and the coveted Empire.

After the Confederacy had been formed he was sent abroad as an ambassador to invite recognition and assistance from the monarchical powers of Europe, but as those powers would not entertain the recognition of the Confederacy with slavery as an acknowledged feature of its foundation, and while he and his followers would have willingly sacrificed slavery if such sacrifice would bring about the establishing of the Gulf Empire, they clearly foresaw that the sacrificing of slavery to obtain European recognition of the Confederacy would only end in driving most of the States back into the Union, where, under Mr. Lincoln's guarantee, slavery where it existed would receive protection, he gave up the cause as lost, ran the blockade, returned home disheartened and took his seat in the Confederate Senate. He died in comparative obscurity.

Without elaborating the subject after giving you these imperfect pictures of two prominent revolutionists, I will only state that from all I saw and from all I heard, the conclusions I arrived at was that Imperialism was the motive for Secession.

III.

PREPARATIONS FOR WAR—THE FIRST TROOPS TO RESPOND.

THE dark, impenetrable clouds, so long gathering, enshrouding the fate of popular government, growing more threatening as they deepened, were on the 13th of April, 1861, lightened up by the flashes from rebel guns in Charleston harbor, which at once dispelled all doubts as to the nature of the storm that was to sweep over the land. The effect was an instantaneous uprising of the people to defend the heritage of the fathers.

From farm to hamlet, hamlet to town, and town to city, the embers of patriotism were fanned into a blaze. There is no period in this country's history which is marked with a purer, more unselfish patriotism than that embraced in the days intervening the 13th of April and the 1st of May, 1861, and no spot that witnessed its fuller display than the Commonwealth of Pennsylvania.

Andrew Gregg Curtin, forty-four years of age, whose election in October, 1860, insured that of Mr.

Preparations for War.

Lincoln to the Presidency in the November following, occupied the Governor's chair at Harrisburg.

Being absent from the State at the time of his nomination for Governor, I have no personal knowledge of the forces which accomplished that result, but there was evident partisan wisdom in the selection, as he was, perhaps, the very strongest candidate his party could have named.

Pennsylvania was the pivotal State and its October election the pivot upon which turned the indicating arm pointing to party success in the Union. It was undoubtedly true that notwithstanding the division in the Democratic ranks, Mr. Lincoln's success depended largely, if not wholly, upon his party carrying the State of Pennsylvania for Governor in October. Party necessity therefore both demanded and commanded the stifling of personal jealousies and ambitions among the leaders and in the party ranks, and the selection of a standard-bearer who throughout the contest would fearlessly bear aloft its banner. Curtin was chosen, and the result proved the wisdom of the choice. He was richly endowed with all those physical qualities necessary to make up a full development of a handsome man. To these were added a well-stored, well-balanced brain; a thorough knowledge of the history of the Commonwealth and its resources; a full fund of language which flowed from his lips with magnetic attraction in a copious, unbroken stream. Earnest in intent and prompt in action, he was the very personification of an ideal leader of the people. With strong convictions on all questions that agitated the public mind, he was moderate in the language he used in giving expression to them, and in consequence did not invite any violent antagonisms. With an energy and a zeal that would not permit him to entertain any other idea than that of success, he took up the burdens of the campaign and addressed the people in almost every city and county of the State.

His classic oratory, resounding throughout the valleys and re-echoing from the hills, vibrated the grand old Commonwealth with music rarely heard.

The people, regardless of former political affiliations, attracted to his standard and enthused by his speeches, triumphantly elected him over a worthy, pure and able opponent by an astonishing majority.

The war cloud had burst, the flood gates opened, and the stream of blood began to flow.

The proclamation of the President, dated April 15, 1861, calling for militia from the various States to suppress the combinations in the South then defying the laws of the United States, reached Harrisburg by telegraph on the morning of that date. This was followed by a telegram from Secretary of War Simon Cameron, notifying the Governor that Pennsylvania's quota under the call would be sixteen regiments, two of which were wanted in Washington within two days, as the enemies of the Government were seriously threatening that city, which was almost entirely unprotected, and that the means for its defense were inadequate. The Governor, without issuing any formal proclamation, telegraphed that of the President to every telegraph station and county town in the State, subjoining an appeal of his own full of patriotic fire, resolve and enthusiastic suggestion. The immediate practical response was found in the reporting at Harrisburg before the morning of the 18th of five full companies of uniformed militia.

The Ringgold Light Artillery, Captain James McKnight, of Reading, was the first to arrive at 8 p. m. of the 16th, closely followed by the Logan Guards, Captain John B. Selheimer, of Lewistown, who arrived two hours later. The National Light Infantry, Captain Edmund McDonald, of Pottsville, the Washington Artillery, Captain James Wren, of Pottsville, and the Allen Guard, Captain Yeager, of Allentown, arrived at one time, 8 p. m. of the 17th.

On the arrival of the Ringgold Artillery at Harrisburg, Capt. McKnight reported at the State Headquarters for orders, but the Governor being absent in Washington, orders could not be obtained from that source. The Captain, not to be checked in his patriotic ardor, telegraphed to Washington for them, and in reply received instruction from Secretary Cameron to proceed to Washington by the first train. These instructions were not obeyed because the official family of the Governor were confronted with, to them, the grave proposition that the militia of the State could not be moved beyond the State's borders and into and through another State without involving it in conflict with the authorities and people of the latter; and Eli Slifer, Secretary of the Commonwealth, representing the Governor, instructed Capt. McKnight to delay his departure for Washington until he should receive his orders from the Governor. Although from all parts of the Commonwealth could be heard the steady tread of its sons as they hastened to enroll themselves for the defense and perpetuation of Constitutional government, the movement of troops towards Washington for that city's relief was halted until the early morning of the 18th, when Fitz John Porter arriving at Harrisburg cut, to the entire approbation of Governor Curtin, who had returned to the Capital, the constitutional knot, by ordering the militia to be mustered into the United States service and to move as United States troops. By 9 a. m., Porter had these five companies, comprising 482 officers and men, mustered into the service of the United States, loaded on board a Northern Central Railway train and started for Washington. They had for company on the train forty-five regulars of the 4th Artillery en route for Fort McHenry, under command of Captain J. C. Pemberton, that recreant son of Pennsylvania who, deserting the flag of his country, joined the Southern Confederacy, became one of its Lieut. Generals, and is now only known to fame as having unconditionally surrendered his command at Vicksburg to General Ulysses S. Grant.

The trip was uneventful until Baltimore was reached. There, on account of the hostile attitude of a large part of the population, who had the sympathy and encouragement of many people of wealth and influence, as well as that of the active portion of the police authorities, it was deemed prudent to disembark at Bolton, a station on the outskirts of the city, and march the command for two miles to Camden Station, on the Baltimore and Ohio Railroad, where it was again to take a train for Washington. The march was a most perilous one. From the moment the command disembarked it was followed and attacked by as desperate a mob as ever passion raised. The mob multiplied as it moved, filling the air with the noise of its threatenings, its oaths and its imprecations. But, regardless of their surroundings, and with minds intent on their mission, the little band of devoted patriots, without a word of reply or a movement towards defense, marched unflinchingly on. As the passions and demonstrations of the mob increased with its numbers so the determination of the patriots increased as dangers accumulated around them and they pushed steadily forward until Camden Station was entered. At that point the mob, fully ten thousand strong, infuriated by the cool and intrepid demeanor of the command, broke through all restraint and began a fierce assault upon it with brickbats, bottles, stones and other like missiles. Amid a storm of that character the command embarked upon the train in waiting. The mob then attempted to detach the engine from the train, but the resolute engineer supported by the crew held the mob at bay with drawn revolvers until they had the train beyond the reach of assault.

This patriotically-inspired march of the five companies of Pennsylvanians through Baltimore was one of the most fearless incidents of the civil war.

With the exception of thirty-four muskets, for which there was no ammunition, the arms of the officers, the sabres of the artillery and one box of percussion caps, they had no means of defense as they made their march through what was practically a hostile camp. That they run the fearful gauntlet with no injuries but slight cuts and bruises received at Camden Station was due solely to their manly courage, self-control, determined bearing, and last, but not least, the sustaining consciousness of performing duty. They arrived in Washington a little after sundown, the first installment of that grand army of citizen soldiery which was so soon to follow and which was destined, mid the din and carnage of war, to render illustrious the American name and to establish the indestructibility of the American Republic.

On the afternoon of the 17th I ran telegraph wires into the Executive Chamber, and there, with a key and a relay, established on a window sill the first electric telegraph office for military purposes on this continent.

On the 18th the alarms momentarily coming from Washington as to its danger, and the very threatening attitude of Baltimore, caused the Governor and his civil and military family extreme uneasiness as to the fate in store for the gallant five companies essaying to reach Washington. With almost breathless impatience they hung over the little instrument, drinking in with avidity every word relating to the movement of the command. When the companies had reached Baltimore and the perils surrounding them became known, the Governor and his assistants deserted my improvised office and made haste to the *Commercial* office down town, as if they would be nearer to the boys. At that office they received with deepest solicitude the details of the march as they were being revealed. The hour was a gloomy one filled with the darkest forebodings. Therefore, great was the relief when the telegraph announced that the command was safely out of Baltimore and speeding towards Washington. With this experience before him the Governor on his return to the Executive Chamber vowed that no more Pennsylvania troops should move to the front unless they were properly armed and equipped to defend themselves, a vow he faithfully kept.

Here let me narrate an incident that occurred in my presence which illustrated the status of Curtin in his relation to the conduct of the war.

Early one morning in the latter part of April, 1861, there came into the Executive Chamber an agent accredited from Governor Andrews, of Massachusetts, to Governor Curtin, who announced his mission to be the obtaining of permission from the latter allowing a son of John Brown, of Harper's Ferry notoriety, to pass through Pennsylvania with a selected company of men, recruiting secretly on the way enroute to Virginia for the purpose of causing an uprising of the slaves against their masters.

As the horrors of a servile insurrection, in which innocent women and children would be the chief victims, loomed up before him, Curtin seemed paralyzed for a moment at the cold-blooded proposition. Then, recovering himself, his frame quivering with majestic anger, his tones surcharged with indignation, he dismissed the agent, saying, "No! I will not permit John Brown's son to pass through Pennsylvania for such a purpose, but I will use the whole power of the Commonwealth to prevent his doing so. Go! tell those who sent you here that so far as I am concerned this war will be conducted only by civilized methods."

But why eulogize Curtin and Pennsylvania's soldiers further? His patriotic actions and their heroic deeds have passed into imperishable history upon whose pages they shine with a spotless lustre.

It is a fact rarely known or commented upon,

that to Pennsylvania belongs the honor not only of sending the first troops to the assistance of Washington in 1861, but also of tendering to the Government, for the defense of the Union, the first organized body of men. This offer went from the National Light Infantry of Pottsville, Edmund McDonald, Captain commanding, April 11, 1861, and reached the War Department April 13th, in response to the enemies' guns which had opened on the flag at Sumter. The offer was immediately accepted. I have yet to learn that any other single company was accepted by the Government during the war. The following certificate, written by Simon Cameron, is of interest in this connection:

"PHILADELPHIA, July 4, 1866.

"I certify that the Pottsville National Light Infantry was the first company of volunteers whose services were offered for the defense of the Capital. A telegram reached the War Department on the 13th making the tender. It was immediately accepted. The company reached Washington on the 18th of April, 1861, with four additional companies from Pennsylvania, and these were the first troops to reach the seat of Government at the beginning of the war of the rebellion.

"SIMON CAMERON."

General Cameron erred in stating the offer was made by telegraph. It was sent by mail as above noted.

IV.

THE COCKEYSVILLE CAMPAIGN AND FITZ JOHN PORTER.

WHILE the five Pennsylvania companies were making their way to Washington a large force of the people were gathering at Harrisburg. They came as individuals, in squads and by companies, and in a short time a large body had arrived, changing the appearance of the town from that of a peaceful, quiet capital into a noisy, armed camp. By the events of the 19th of April, wherein Baltimore treason displayed its ferocity by murdering troops on their way to Washington and by tearing up railroads, burning bridges and cutting down telegraph wires, thus isolating Washington City from the North, it became necessary to hurriedly organize the arriving hosts. Unaccustomed to military affairs it is not surprising that the people of the North were filled with consternation as they saw the capital of the country cut off from all communication with them and likely to fall at any moment into the hands of the enemies to the Government by direct attack or surely to fall within a fortnight from starvation. Nor is it surprising that there were distracted, divided, although patriotic, counsels. It was fortunate that at this time there was in Harrisburg a man in whom the civil authorities could rely, and upon whom they could lean. That man was Fitz John Porter, born in New Hampshire in September, 1822. He was educated at West Point, where he graduated in 1845 as a brevet second lieutenant in the Fourth Artillery. In 1847 he was promoted to a first lieutenant, and was with his regiment as it moved with General Scott in his conquest of the City of Mexico.

He was conspicuously gallant at the battles of Melino del Rey, Chapultepec, and the Garita de Belen, receiving respectively the brevet ranks of captain and major for his conduct. At the last-named battle he was severely wounded. Subsequent to the peace he was instructor and adjutant at West Point. In 1856, receiving promotion to a captaincy in the Adjutant General's department, he gave up his line rank. When the civil war broke out he was a captain and an Assistant Adjutant General. General Scott and Secretary Cameron, feeling that the Capital was in great danger and that communication between it and the North might be cut off at any moment, selected

Major Porter as an able, true and discreet officer to send to Harrisburg for the purpose of representing the Government in its military arm, of hurrying forward relief, and, if the urgency demanded it, officially using their names and authority without first communicating with them. It was a trust well reposed and faithfully executed.

Porter was a man of unquestioned courage, undoubted ability, and exalted patriotism. He was not a magnetic man in the sense of creating noisy enthusiasm in troops whenever he appeared, but he was magnetic in attracting and holding the absolute confidence of all men under and around him. To his coolness and intrepidity in action was added a keen, penetrating mind that enabled him to judge rapidly and correctly.

His arrival at Harrisburg was opportune and his services there invaluable to the authorities and Government. He at once set the military machinery in motion and by April 20 had organized and mustered into the United States service the First Regiment Pennsylvania Volunteers, Col. Samuel Yohe, and despatched it that night as the advance of an army to move through Baltimore to reopen communication with Washington. The companies comprising the Second Regiment were mustered on the same day, but the regimental organization was not perfected until the 21st, when Frederick C. Stumbach was chosen colonel. That night Major Porter despatched this regiment to join the First and Third who were then in the neighborhood of Cockeysville, a station on the Northern Central Railway, about fifteen miles northwest of Baltimore.

The Third Regiment under Col. Francis P. Minier had been organized, mustered and despatched on the 20th. The three regiments were under the general command of Brigadier General Geo. C. Wynkoop. They were of the very best material, intelligent, brave and patriotic, but exceedingly deficient in military knowlege, the militia of the State being only a military organization in name and form. What military knowledge then existed in the command was confined to the few survivors of the Mexican war who formed a component part of the several regiments. This knowlege was not of much avail in the exigencies which had arisen and Major Porter had his hands full.

After Wynkoop's command arrived in Cockeysville, Porter, seeing the necessity of having a support to it that would inspire confidence, was hastily organizing a body of regular cavalry under Major Geo. H. Thomas. Porter in person arrived at Cockeysville

Fitz John Porter.

late in the morning of April 21 and was met by Col. Richard Delafield and Capt. Daniel Tyler of the regular army, who aided in giving confidence to General Wynkoop, and instructions to him and his subordinates. He had expected to have been able on his arrival to order a forward march on Baltimore, but was disappointed in not finding at Cockeysville either Major Thomas' command, Sherman's Battery of Artillery, nor the organized party of road and bridge repairers he had provided for and expected to meet.

As all prudent counsel and calm judgment indicated that to prevent bloodshed in making the repairs to the railway and in effecting the passage of Baltimore the command should be accompanied by regular troops, Major Porter after properly disposing of the troops and giving orders to General Wynkoop hastily returned to Harrisburg to expedite the movement of the regulars. So successful were his efforts that by sundown he had embarked under Major Thomas four hundred dismounted cavalry, and a force of bridge builders with bridge material. Taking passage with the former he arrived at York about midnight, expecting to reach Cockeysville in abundant time to move the column early on the morning of the 22nd. But here occurred one of those singular circumstances which frequently happened in the subsequent years of the war—a countermanding of orders at the critical moment when success depended upon the original orders being carried out. The onward movement of Major Porter's train was stopped by the notice of an arriving locomotive with orders from Washington to stop the advance of the troops on Baltimore, and directing their return to Pennsylvania to be forwarded via Philadelphia and Annapolis. Major James Belger, of the Quartermaster's Department, was said to be the bearer of the orders and empowered to carry them out. Major Porter was dumfounded, could not believe that such orders would be issued, and much less that an officer of the Quartermaster's Department would be detailed to carry out such a strategic movement. Not seeing the orders, he resisted to the extent of his ability the execution of them. The railroad was practically in the hands of Major Belger, and the railroad officials would not move Major Porter southward without first knowing that the track was clear to warrant such movement with safety. The telegraph line was so frequently interrupted south of York that it was impossible to obtain any reliable information upon which to base action, and so wore the night away;

but when the dawn of the 22nd broke it disclosed the troops from Cockeysville on board of arriving trains at York. With the trains came Major Belger and the orders. The latter were, first an order from the Secretary of War, by direction of the President, to return the troops then near Cockeysville, Md., to York, Pa., and directing the officer in charge to leave sufficient force along the railroad to keep it safe from depredations and within his entire control; the second, an order from General Winfield Scott to return the troops to Harrisburg, and forward them from thence via Philadelphia and Annapolis, placing the execution of the order in the hands of Major Belger and abandoning the line of the Northern Central Railway.

On the back of the first order, Secretary Cameron made an endorsement in lead pencil as follows: "Since writing the within order it has been changed by the Lieutenant General by direction of the President. I now add that I direct the railroad to be kept open at all hazards so as to give to the United States the power to send troops or munitions if the necessity for bringing them by that route shall occur by the failure or inability of the Mayor of Baltimore to keep his faith with the President." Both of these orders were issued at the instance of the

President after repeated interviews with the Mayor and prominent citizens of Baltimore, and from a desire to prevent bloodshed in that city. The lead pencil memorandum of Secretary Cameron was written under these circumstances: Major Belger was on his way to the depot in Washington with the original orders when Secretary Cameron met him. The Secretary had been reflecting upon the importance of getting the troops to Washington and of keeping open the line of the Northern Central Railway and hurriedly, as he sat in his carriage, made the memorandum and then verbally directed Major Belger to tell Major Porter to bring on the troops at all hazards. Belger, however, disregarded the Secretary of War's orders, did not deliver the verbal order to Major Porter, but, abandoning the railway to its fate, carried out the Lieutenant General's instructions and took the command out of Porter's hands. It was not until years afterwards that Porter heard of Cameron's verbal orders to him, and that Cameron learned from Belger himself that he had not delivered the orders to Porter.

Thus ended the Cockeysville campaign. Because he did not hold the Pennsylvania troops at Cockeysville, and did not force his way through to Washington with them and the regulars under Major

Thomas, Major Fitz John Porter had for years afterwards the enmity of Secretary Chase, Senators Chandler, Wade and Henry Wilson, the latter acknowledging in after years that that was the first cause of his opposition to him. This seed of opposition grew in secret, and developed into such force that when military incapacity, engrafted upon military jealousy, demanded a sacrifice the powerful partisans threw their weight of partisanism into the scale and deprived this brilliant, this guiltless, this distinguished officer of his well-earned laurels and the Government of his valuable services.

The acts of Fitz John Porter as recorded in the foregoing sketches were not the least of his invaluable services to the Government at that period. Under almost insurmountable difficulties he had with perfect judgment brought out from Texas the only troops saved from Twiggs' surrender and so placed them that they would render the greatest service; he detailed them to the garrisons at Tortugas and Key West, thus not only strengthening but making perfectly safe those positions. As the clouds were darkening, and knowing that Col. Gardner, commandant at Fort Moultrie, was too old to bear the responsibilities which were sure to fall upon him in that command, he selected and caused the appointment of Major Robert Anderson for the post. Anderson's policy was settled in New York in a conference between himself, General Scott and Porter, the latter marking out the plan by which Moultrie was to be evacuated and Sumter occupied and held. Had reinforcements been sent as the plan provided Sumter would have been held. This conference and its agreements were kept secret from the administration at the request of General Scott, because the administration had not sought and was not seeking his advice.

Porter, in addition to his experience in the intestine troubles in Utah and Texas, had cautiously gathered a fund of information useful to the Government, and was now at Harrisburg with communication cut off with the authorities, assuming the most weighty responsibilities. His labors were ceaseless by day and by night. For a week at a time he could not spare a moment to even change his clothing beyond renewing his collars and cuffs.

To enter into all the details of his work, in his seizing the reins and in rousing the people and government officials to the gravity of the crisis, would require a volume of writing. Space herein will not permit, but there was one act so prompt, so proper and so far reaching in its results, that it will always stand as a monument to his ability, fidelity and patriotism. Missouri was in a state of ferment. St. Louis was apparently in the hands of the Secessionists. In the St. Louis Arsenal there were 70,000 stand of arms that the Secessionists were preparing to seize. Missouri Union Volunteers were coming to the front and Lieut. J. M. Schofield, Third Artillery, then in St. Louis, had been detailed to muster them in. General Harney, commanding the District, standing upon what he considered neutral ground, refused to allow the Missouri Unionists to remain in the Arsenal grounds nor to be armed. It was a critical moment, and Frank P. Blair, Jr., using the telegraph office at East St. Louis, sent the following telegram which I received at Harrisburg early in the morning of the day it was dated:

"ST. LOUIS, April 21, 1861.
" *To Governor A. G. Curtin:*
" An officer of the army here has received an order to muster in Missouri regiments. General Harney refuses to let them remain in the arsenal grounds or permit them to be armed. I wish these facts to be communicated to the Secretary of War by special messenger and instructions sent immediately to Harney to receive the troops at the arsenal and arm them. Our friends distrust Harney very much. He should be superceded immediately by putting an-

other commander in the district. The object of the Secessionists is to seize the arsenal here with its seventy thousand stand of arms, and he refuses the means of defending it. We have plenty of men, but no arms.

[Signed] "FRANK P. BLAIR, JR."

Governor Curtin, appreciating the gravity of the situation, which was increased by the certainty that it would require from two to three days' time to perfect full communication with the Secretary of War, and, believing that the delay of an hour might place St. Louis in the hands of the insurgents, turned to Porter and delivered Blair's appeal to him. Major Porter, without a moment's hesitation, used the name of Lieutenant General Winfield Scott and telegraphed Captain N. Lyon, Second Infantry, then at St. Louis, to muster in the Union troops and to use them for the protection of public property. He also notified Harney of the detail and instructed him to see that the troops so mustered should be properly armed and equipped. Telegrams of the same import were sent to Captain Seth Williams, A. A. G., and to the commanding officer of the arsenal at St. Louis, and in the name of the Secretary of War (Simon Cameron) to Mr. Blair.

The prompt receipt of these orders enabled Gen-

Fitz John Porter.

eral Blair, Captain Lyon and other prominent Union men to become masters of the situation, to the entire discomfiture of the Secessionists who by the delay of one day would have been enabled to capture the arsenal, with its valuable contents, and hold St. Louis. General Blair always held that this action of Porter saved Missouri to the Union with all the great benefit to the National cause that such result implied. These few bold and prompt strokes of Porter's pen saved that which had it been lost at the time would have required a large army, with its attendant expense of blood and treasure, months if not years to recover.

Porter, with drawn sword on the Peninsula and on the itineracy of the Army of the Potomac which ended with the battle of Antietam, was an heroic figure, but Porter in the emergency, cut off from all communication with superior authority, standing isolated, pen in hand winning a great and bloodless victory for his country, is a grand character.

V.

BULL RUN TO ANTIETAM.

Dedicated to the memory of Thomas A. Scott, who, in life, whether in times of war or in times of peace, was a foremost citizen in defending his country's rights and advancing its prosperity.

THE battle of Bull Run and its attending disasters threw the country into a great turmoil of excitement. The loyal people were appalled when the startling fact broke upon them that they had vastly underrated the strength, power and resources of the enemy. They saw that they were sadly disappointed in their supposition that the army of raw levies from the workshops, fields, counters and offices of the North, accustomed only to the avocations of peace, would, in three short months, whip a military people, fighting under the stimulus of desperation.

"Bull Run" was an error which a round of circumstances made the Government commit. The three months' enlistments were drawing to the end of the term; the troops not satisfied with the great work they had performed of saving the Capitol, desired a taste of war's bitter fruits in the frenzied fray; influences from civil life clamored for a battle, and everywhere throughout the land the cry of "On to Richmond" could be heard; capitalists who had loaned the Government their wealth, Senators and Representatives in Congress who had the voting of supplies, and the radical abolitionists with an impetuousness inborn of their detestation of slavery, demanded a demonstration against the enemy. The President at last gave way under the pressure thus brought to bear upon him and added his voice to the throng in urging an onward movement. Long and fervent were the remonstrances of the veteran General Scott and the young and intrepid McDowell, but they, too, had to give way to the noisy clamors, and the consequence was an order for McDowell to advance his army on Manassas, the stronghold of the enemy. The result, that toughly-contested battle, fought on a hot Sunday, which brought so much distress, dismay and disgrace to the arms of the Union.

While the action was progressing I was on duty in the War Department at Washington as military telegraph operator, and around me was gathered one of the most illustrious groups brought together during the war with the Confederate States, to witness on that beautiful Sunday the tragedy being enacted on the banks of Bull Run.

Military science, surrendered to the passions of the people, had passed under newspaper and partisan political control, and the group had gathered to watch the practical effects of that surrender, little dreaming what the declining of that day's sun would disclose.

The group was composed of President Lincoln, William H. Seward, Simon Cameron, Salmon P. Chase, Gideon Welles and Edward Bates, of the Cabinet; Colonels Townsend, Van Rensalaer, Hamilton and Wright, of General Scott's staff; General Mansfield, commanding the defenses of Washington, and Col. Thomas A. Scott, of Pennsylvania. With maps of the field before them they watched, as it were, the conflict of arms as it progressed, at the same time keeping up a running desultory conversation.

The military telegraph, which had not yet reached the efficiency which afterwards characterized it, extended only to Fairfax Court House, from which point General McDowell kept the authorities advised of his movements. Hour after hour the couriers reported unbrokenly that our troops were steadily forcing the enemy back, but as that was expected, the reports only tended to increase the complacent satisfaction with which all of the party seemed to be possessed.

A despatch had been received from General Robert Patterson, the evening before, announcing that Johnston had eluded him, but the sanguine feeling which animated the group was in no wise abated by that knowledge or by the probability of Johnston forming a junction with Beauregard that day.

The day passed quietly in the Department, all present looking forward with an abiding confidence for McDowell's success.

Mr. Lincoln, deeply impressed with the responsibilities of the occasion, wore a quiet dignity and his observations on the pending conflict were free from humor and were few and measured.

Mr. Seward, complacently smoking a cigar, displayed a consciousness that his prophecy of a thirty days' war was about being verified.

Mr. Cameron, not doubting the result of the day's work, yet not sharing in Mr. Seward's views as to the duration of the war with the forces then in hand, gave expression to his opinions in the forcible, practical manner for which he was distinguished.

The military gentlemen explained movements, besides occasionally withdrawing themselves for the purpose of advising General Scott of the battle's progress, he being too much enfeebled by the infirmities of age to leave his quarters.

The other gentlemen of the group were deeply interested observers.

Up to half-past three o'clock in the afternoon advices from McDowell were frequent, the despatches at that hour indicating that he was pressing Beauregard back to Manassas Junction. From then on until the shades of evening were drawing on apace an ominous silence settled upon the telegraph. The conversation of the gentlemen took a speculative turn on the causes of the sudden cessation of information from the field, the generally expressed opinion being that McDowell, flushed with victory, was too busily engaged in securing its fruits to write despatches. But as time wore on, and speculation had almost given way to impatience, the throbbing instrument broke its long silence and told that "Our army is retreating." Such information being entirely unexpected, was received at first with incredulity, but as corroboration soon followed, and the fact became apparent that the army was not only retreating but was flying in a panic, it was received and accepted with outward composure. There was no consternation and but a feeble ripple of excitement of momentary duration and scarcely discernible. As the result was the opposite of the anticipations, it would be expected that the sudden revulsion would have at least produced great excitement, but whatever may have been the thoughts and feelings of these gentlemen they kept them closely veiled as the truth was being revealed. Mr. Seward smoked on without the slightest perturbation being shown upon his countenance, in his manner or speech. The days of his prophecy were ended, and he extricated himself from the consequences of their not bringing fulfilment by extending them to a later period. Colonel Thomas A. Scott, turning to General Mansfield, said, quietly, "General, it would be well to man your fortifications and stay this retreat," and then left the Department with Mr. Cameron for the purpose of holding a consultation with General Scott. As the telegraph reported the terrible scenes and heartrending stories of sufferings during the progress of that never-to-be-forgotten flight, Mr. Lincoln felt that the hour of the Nation's greatest peril was opening, and while making preparations to meet it, the saddened lines of his countenance deepened and his whole soul seemed to go out in sympathy to the dying, the sick and wounded, the foot-sore and the weary.

General Scott could not understand that a "hero of one hundred battles" could be beaten, and he only believed when the advancing hurricane of the flying, panic-stricken army sounded its approach to the Capital. When the veteran at last believed he gave me an autograph order to suppress all news of the disaster which might be offered for telegraphing to the country. Armed with this document I drove down Pennsylvania avenue to the American Telegraph office and notified its manager of the commands of the General-in-Chief. Piled upon the telegraph tables were "specials" from the field describing, in thrilling language—as only the "War Correspondent" could describe—the scenes and events of the day. All intimations of disaster were ruthlessly cut from the specials, and only the rose-coloring permitted to be telegraphed. Thus it was that while the gloom of the darkest hour in the Republic's history hung like a pall over Washington City, throughout the North bells were ringing out rejoicings over the glad tidings of victory.

Telegrams were sent to General McClellan, at Beverly, in Western Virginia, informing him of a "repulse" to McDowell, and to Generals Banks and Dix—both of whom were in Baltimore—instructing them to keep their men under arms. No official telegrams for aid were sent at this time, but Colonel Thomas A. Scott, with a keen perception of the situation, and foreseeing the necessities of the morrow, sent a telegram to Governor Curtin, at Harrisburg, which, in conception and composition, was so characteristic of the man who no sooner saw a want than he comprehended its supply, that I give its entire text here:

"WASHINGTON, July 21, 1861.
"*Hon. A. G. Curtin, Harrisburg, Pa.:*
"Get your regiments at Harrisburg, Easton and other points ready for immediate shipment; lose no time in preparing; make things move to the utmost.
[Signed] "THOMAS A. SCOTT."

This despatch anticipated, by many hours, any official action looking towards a call for " more troops." The reply to it was found in the hastening of the famous Pennsylvania Reserves to the relief of the threatened Capital. Mr. Lincoln lingered around the War Department until about two o'clock in the morning, when he retired to the White House, leaving Mr. Scott on guard, an active, watchful sentinel of the movements of the night. Had the country been consulted, there could not have been selected from among its patriotic sons, an abler, truer, wiser, braver guardian, than the noble Pennsylvanian whom Mr. Lincoln left on guard to care for its interests in the crisis which had come upon it.

At the close of the battle of Bull Run, Washington

City was crowded with a disorganized, demoralized mob, scarcely controllable, which had taken the shortest routes from the battle-field to the Capital. The most of the persons composing it were eagerly demanding their discharges, as the term of their enlistments had either expired or were expiring. It was indeed a dark day that had fallen upon the country. While a strong and victorious enemy, jubilant over its success, was threatening the very gates of the Capital, its defenders, scattered and unmanageable, were parading the streets and avenues in grotesque parties spinning yarns of individual valor.

General Simon Cameron held the portfolio of the Department of War. He was assisted by Colonel Thomas A. Scott, one of the best-equipped and practical minds of the day, a man whose energy and applicability enabled him to surmount any difficulty that might be thrown in his way.

At a consultation held immediately after the battle, it was determined upon bringinging the young military chieftain, General McClellan, from the scene of his successes in Western Virginia to reorganize the army for the defense of the Union. With his prestige, ability and ardor he soon brought order out of chaos, and had a large army in training on the banks of

Bull Run to Antietam.

the Potomac. A perfect net-work of fortifications sprang up around Washington at the hands of accomplished and experienced engineers. Daily troops were formed into beautiful human machines whose every movement betokened harmony of action. Colonel Lorenzo Thomas was made, by brevet, a Brigadier General, and occupied the post of Adjutant General; Captain Meigs, an eminent engineer, whose work upon the Washington aqueduct and the dome of the Capitol had given him a world-wide reputation, was appointed Quartermaster General, with the rank of brevet Brigadier General; Colonel J. W. Ripley, advanced to similar rank, was promoted to Chief of the Bureau of Ordnance, and Colonel Joseph Taylor, brother of old "Rough and Ready," acted as Commissary General of Subsistence.

The army, under the auspices of these learned military men, became, as it were, an army of veterans, ever ready for the fray in which they might retrieve the Nation's honor and punish treason. The summer wore away in bringing the army into condition and insuring the invulnerability of the political metropolis of the country, and just as the frosts of autumn had rendered an advance upon the enemy practicable, rains set in, causing Virginia's proverbially bad roads to become perfectly impassable.

Rains continued throughout the fall and winter. Roads had no bottoms, and the ground became so thoroughly saturated that at the close of 1861 and the commencement of 1862, regimental and even company drill had to be abandoned. The pickets in camp and on the outposts, stationed in the most advantageous positions, unable to *walk* their posts, plodded them, and that often through mud to their ankles. The only consolation our troops gave themselves in their mud-bound condition was that of believing the enemy were in no better condition. The only difference which did exist was, that while our army, ever prepared for an advance, waited for propitious weather in tents, the enemy had gone into comparatively comfortable winter quarters.

During the time the Grand Army of the Potomac lay thus inactive, independent movements were made and large drafts for the men to carry them into effect were made upon it. These movements and depletions of his ranks were strenuously opposed by General McClellan, on the ground of bad policy. He contended that while it weakened his army the advantages arising from striking at and occupying isolated points in the South could in no way be equal to those that would arise from his bearing down with a large and overwhelming force upon the positions where the strength of the enemy was centered. Further, that concentration, not the isolation, of divisions was the true principle upon which the war should be conducted, to bring the rebellion to a speedy conclusion. This sage and deep reasoning was overthrown, and he was compelled to see some of his choicest troops taken away from him, but to his honor and patriotism be it said, that the moment the policy of independent movements were resolved upon, he gave all his talents and energy to ensure their success.

The retiracy of General Winfield Scott, in the fall of 1861, caused the appointment of McClellan as General Commanding the United States Army. Multiplied as his duties became, by reason of his advancement, he did not shrink an instant from the responsibilities of his position, but went to work with an energy which soon infused new life into the whole army. He planned his campaign, then set to work in bringing his combination to perfection. Day and night have I seen him busily engaged moving the vast machinery of the whole army and personally attending to the details of the management of his immediate command—the great Army of the Potomac. Not a moment of time did he devote to himself excepting such hours as nature demanded for repose, and those he curtailed to the utmost limit. His meals were oftenest eaten while he labored. A little wicker basket, containing a few sandwiches, some bread and cheese, and now and then a tart, was the storehouse from which for days he drew his only provisions. The results of his excessive labors and close confinement to duty were shown, in colors of brilliancy, by the gallant achievements in the West, the restoration of Kentucky and Tennessee to the Union, the evacuation of Manassas and Corinth, the reopening of the Mississippi and the occupation of New Orleans.

These glorious results were clearly attributable to the genius of McClellan, and would have been the forerunner of greater achievements, bringing the war to a close, with a restored Union, within eighteen months from the time Sumter was fired upon, had he been allowed to pursue his plans to their final consummation. It was not to be so. Simon Cameron resigned as Secretary of War, and Edwin M. Stauton was appointed his successor. From that moment the policy of the Department of War changed. Mr. Stanton had a national reputation of being an eminent legal scholar, withal he was ambitious to unhealthiness, egotistic, bombastic, arrogant and untruthful. He was called upon to act in a department, the highly patriotic duties of which he was entirely unfitted for. It was peculiarly unfortunate that Mr. Lincoln's foresightedness should have failed him when he consented to the appointment of Stanton. We can only lament that it did. The fulsome laudation of the press of the country soon raised Stanton to a standard far beyond his caliber, and the people, so prone to allow their enthusiasm to carry their judgment beyond the line of prudence, carried the standard to a more giddy height, so that Stanton, looking in any direction, saw nothing but himself. His egoism and vanity were catered to, causing him to assume the position he did which proved so disastrous to the country. His incapacity to wield the scepter placed in his hands soon showed itself.

Simon Cameron and Thomas A. Scott, unaided, had performed all the necessary administrative work of the Department in raising, equipping, organizing and placing in the field an army of six hundred thousand men, besides receiving and hearing the large crowds of people who, in rapid streams, flowed into Washington from all quarters of the country. Day and night they were accessible to any person that might call upon them. Mark the effect of the change. Secretary Cameron's resignation took place when the army was ready to move and the business of the Department had dwindled down to mere routine. Notwithstanding this, Mr. Stanton insisted upon having three Assistant Secretaries of War and a large addition to his corps of clerks, and after receiving that additional assistance, he denied audiences four days in the week to all callers, the President and members of the Cabinet alone excepted. On the remaining two days he graciously permitted access to his presence, designating five hours of one day as the time for Senators and members of Congress and five hours of the other day as the time for the general public and officers of the army to call.

The atmosphere of the Department soon thickened with the atoms of autocracy and snobbery, erstwhile found flying around the heads of royalty, but which now had effected a lodgment on and around Mr. Stanton's desk.

The reason announced for the enlargement of the force and curtailment of the freedom of access was that such action was necessary for the expedition of business. If such necessity existed, it was a thousand times more urgent under Cameron than under Stanton; but the fact is that it did not exist at all, and the only reasonable explanation of Stanton's action was to be found in an overwhelming desire on his part to surround himself with a seeming inapproachableness so as to enable him to undo all that had been done by his predecessor. That he succeeded in obtaining his desire is fully attested by subsequent events. Enlistments were stopped, and the ranks of the army, instead of being kept up to a standard of six hundred thousand fighting men, were being reduced daily by sickness and the casualties of war, and no one to fill up the vacant files.

McClellan forced the enemy to abandon his extremely strong position at Manassas, and then sought a new base of operations in the Peninsula. Evacuation by the enemy of Yorktown and the lines of the James, Chicahominy and York rivers to a new position within a few miles from Richmond was an early result. McClellan was thus in a position to realize his fond anticipations of bringing the war to a speedy conclusion, but the policy of the War Department was against him, and it was impossible for him to successfully contend with that enemy in the rear, and the armed foe in the front. The failure of McDowell to form a junction with him, and the non-arrival of needed reinforcements caused the necessity for the change of base to the James river accompanied by the "Seven days' fight" with all its attendant casualties. The President on appeal said every man was sent McClellan that could be sent him; that there were no more to send. That was unquestionably true, but why? Enlistments had been stopped when they should have gone on, at least until such time as would be required to have a sufficient force in reserve for just such emergencies as arose. Cameron's policy would have insured a patriotic army of a million of men, and operations would not have had to be suspended a moment for new levies to be made. Reserves under that policy could have been sent forward to close decimated ranks, enabling a steady advance of the Union columns upon all those spots where the Confederacy had its armed forces. "No men to send" caused Banks to retreat to the Potomac, and laid open to the enemy the beautiful Valley of the Shenandoah. Yet Banks' retreat was not a warning. To be sure it fired the patriotic heart of the country, and caused large bodies of able-bodied men to rush forward and tender their services to the Government, but the Government, under the baneful influence of Stanton and his policy, cooled the ardor of the people by refusing to accept the noble offers, on the pretext that there were sufficient men in the field. Had those sons of constitutional liberty been accepted, Mc-

Clellan could have had an overwhelming force at his command with which to destroy the Southern Army, capture Richmond and close the war.

While McClellan was at Harrison's Landing putting the Army of the Potomac into condition for a movement upon Richmond, and calling for reinforcements that never came, the War Department authorities at Washington were again tampering with the organization of the army. The corps of McDowell, Banks and Fremont, and the garrison of Washington, which had been detached from McClellan's command, were organized into the "Army of Virginia," and placed under command of Major General John Pope, who signalized his incapacity for such duty by boastfully proclaiming in general orders, that the securing of "bases of operations" and "lines of retreat" should be left to the enemy. The enemy promptly secured Pope's. To cap the climax of blundering, if not absolutely criminal stupidity, Major General Henry W. Halleck, who had never marshaled even a squad in the field, was called to Washington as General-in-Chief of the Armies of the United States. Stanton thus became strongly reinforced in the carrying out of his system of undoing, and heartily did Halleck and Pope respond to all calls he made upon them to aid him in that direction. All military maxims were disregarded, and the Army of the Potomac was recalled from the line of the James.

That frightful blunder was immediately taken advantage of by General Lee, who made a bold move to reach Washington by turning its right flank. On the second of August, 1862, General Halleck issued orders for the recall of the Army of the Potomac, and on the ninth of that month General " Stonewall " Jackson's advance of Lee's army had crossed the Rapidan and encountered Banks at Cedar Mountain. Battle after battle followed until they culminated in the disgraceful overthrow of Pope at the very gates of the Capital.

Lee thus cleared his line of communications so that his march through the Shenandoah into the Cumberland Valley should be unimpeded.

The danger to the Capital was imminent, and the Government and the people were thoroughly and completely aroused. By the orders of Stanton and Halleck, McClellan had been despoiled of all command, but when dismay spread its dark mantle over Washington, President Lincoln telegraphed him, "I beg of you to assist me in this crisis, with your ability and experience. I am entirely tired out." And to the utter discomfiture of Stanton and Chase, who would have preferred the surrender of Washington to accepting its safety at the hands of McClellan, placed him at the head of the army for the defense of Washington.

On the 11th of September Longstreet's corps of Lee's army was occupying Hagerstown and vicinity.

McClellan, having hastily reorganized the army, cautiously followed, covering Washington as he progressed.

The North was now aroused, and political intrigue and schemes of personal advancement had to be dropped for the time being.

Pennsylvania, which was threatened with the horrors and devastation of war, made strenuous efforts to resist invasion. Governor Curtin's call upon the people was responded to with alacrity, and soon a large army was gathering on the banks of the Susquehanna. This army was composed principally of the militia. It is somewhat customary to smile when the militia are mentioned in connection with actual war, but the fact cannot be truthfully contradicted that whenever the militia were called out they always filled the part they were called upon to act.

At that time Governor Curtin, having been apprised in advance that Pennsylvania must look out for itself, made the most complete arrangements for the State's defense. He summoned the militia of the Commonwealth to gather at the border, and there await his arrival.

> "Then marched the brave from rocky steep,
> From mountain river swift and cold;
> The borders of the stormy deep,
> The vales where gathered waters sleep,
> Sent up the strong and bold."

They gathered, and I can see them now with their bright guns flashing in the September sunlight; their fresh blouses with shining buttons; their canteens overflowing with the cool waters of the Conococheague, and their haversacks filled with rations. They were a fine sight to behold as their lines were formed in field and wood. Some of them were imbued with State pride and citizen duty to such a high degree that they hesitated in crossing the border for fear that it would be doing an unconstitutional act! This fact coming to the knowledge of Curtin how grand he looked and how magical the effect when he appeared before the doubting ones and informed them that the border line was only an imaginary one, and assured them that wherever Pennsylvania troops would follow, there Pennsylvania's Governor would lead. So it was that, with all the "pride, pomp and circumstance of glorious war," with drums beating and banners waving, they bravely crossed the border. The column marched, and in good time arrived at Hagerstown, where its Chief established his headquarters. It then moved out the Williamsport road, along which it was drawn up in line of battle to meet a portion of the enemy advancing on its front. The position was one of great responsibility and full of danger, and had it not been filled by the militia it would have been necessary to fill it from the Army of the Potomac, then engaged with Lee's main forces. Therefore, although not in the battle of Antietam with its shifting scenes of successes and defeats, its carnage and its glories, the Pennsylvania militia are entitled to great praise for assisting in bringing about its results.

On the 13th of September Longstreet's corps of Lee's army was at Hagerstown, his advance having reached there on the 11th. Hill was at the base of South Mountain, and Jackson was investing Harper's Ferry. General McClellan's headquarters were at Frederick.

McClellan had a three-fold duty to perform: to punish Lee, cover Washington, and to relieve the garrison at Harper's Ferry. This latter duty should not have been imposed upon him, as it weakened his ability to perform the other duties. Harper's Ferry was of no strategic importance, and the attempt to hold it was only to insure the loss of its garrison. McClellan advised its abandonment and the transfer of the troops there to his command. But as usual, it was only for McClellan to suggest a proper movement to cause the War Department to frustrate its accomplishment; so it was that not until September 12th, that the command at Harper's Ferry was placed under McClellan, contingent upon his opening communication with Miles. Jackson's rapid movements to capture Miles had cut off communication with the latter, and it was only after this became an ascertained fact that Halleck placed Miles under McClellan's orders, subject to the first mentioned contingency. McClellan saw the impending disaster to Miles and tried to avert it, but the authority given him in the premises came too late, as subsequent events proved. McClellan now pushed forward rapidly, and on Sunday morning encountered Hill at the Boonsborough pass of the South Mountain. Hill made a gallant stand, and was reinforced during the afternoon from Longstreet's corps. The action was a bloody one, and while the pæans of victory went to McClellan, Hill accomplished a great result in

Bull Run to Antietam.

detaining McClellan long enough to allow Jackson to accomplish the entire discomfiture of Miles, for the next morning that unfortunate officer surrendered 12,520 men, with all the stores and munitions of war at Harper's Ferry, to Jackson.

Jackson was thus enabled to form a junction with Lee and to enter battle with his troops enthused by their victory, while McClellan was handicapped by being deprived of the moral and material support of over twelve thousand additional troops that he should have had with him when the two great armies clashed in battle on the banks of the Antietam.

On the 15th of September McClellan continued his march, and late in the afternoon came up with the enemy near Sharpsburg; but he had not sufficient force at that time to warrant an attack. On the 16th a fog prevailed, and the day was devoted by the gallant antagonists in concentrating their forces, strengthening their lines and manœuvering for position preparatory to the deadly fray so close at hand. Artillery firing was kept up throughout the day, and late in the afternoon Mead's Division, composed of Pennsylvania Reserves, supported by other divisions of Hooker's corps, engaged the enemy in a sharp and bloody conflict to which darkness put a stop.

The 17th opened beautifully, with all the splendor of a September sun reflecting its rays over the scene. As the sunlight broke over the contending forces resting on their arms or marching towards the chosen ground, the great battle of Antietam was begun at the skirmish line of the Pennsylvania Reserves. Soon after regiment upon regiment, brigade upon brigade, division upon division, and corps upon corps, were thrown into action, until not less than one hundred thousand men shared in the glories or suffered in the disasters of the stubborn conflict. From the time of the first firing in the morning until night threw its mantle over the smoke of the field the battle raged with terrific fury, and hope and fear alternated in the breasts of contending sides. Heroism, patriotism and valor wrote their names on history's page all over the sanguinary field which was strewn with nearly twenty-one thousand dead and wounded men—3,620 dead bodies, and 17,365 wounded men attested to the fierceness of the struggle. Neither army could claim a victory in the fight, neither was in a condition to renew the battle next day, but the prestige went to McClellan, because he retained possession of the field. The results, however, were of great importance to the Government. Washington was now safe from attack, and Pennsylvania relieved from threatened invasion.

The reverberations of McClellan's guns at Antietam acclaiming the safety of Washington had not died upon the air before the enemy in the rear, relieved of its fears, again set in motion their system of policy of undoing, and it was not long before McClellan's military career came to an end through their intrigues. Antietam closed the first chapter in the history of the war. Patriotism had thus far triumphed, but from the hour that Lee re-crossed the Potomac, it was placed under a cloud, and partisanship to a greater or less extent controlled the course of subsequent events. Although patriotism was deeply imbedded in the hearts of the army and the people, it was at very low ebb in public places. A new party had come into power, and its followers were not only clamorous for the offices, but they adopted every possible measure to perpetuate their hold on public place, and to put in the background all those who did not vote with them at the polls. No matter how patriotic the citizen, how great were his services and sacrifices for the preservation of the Union, if he did not at once bow his head to the decrees of a partisan caucus he was hounded by the party organ and the petty politician and ostracised from participation in public affairs. There was considerable presidential timber in the Cabinet which was more or less influenced in public action by party clamor. From these causes sprung a spirit of intolerance and intrigue, which, in view of the critical condition the Government found itself in, was akin to treason, that resulted in prolonging the war at a fearful expense of precious life and a vast amount of treasure. Of party men, however, there were a few who were imbued with such broad patriotism that they tried to turn back the tide of intolerance, and to some extent succeeded. Among their number was Simon Cameron. I well remember the morning, in the Secretary of War's office, when Senator King, of New York, came in and reproached Mr. Cameron for appointing Democrats to positions in the army, and Mr. Cameron's reply: "Senator this is not a war for party, it is for the country, and I am with all those who are for the latter." Mr. Cameron never departed from this broad standard of patriotism while he remained in public life. Mr. Lincoln did not partake of the spirit of intolerance, but the radical and intolerant wing of his party were in the majority both in Congress and in his Cabinet, and he was forced at times by the circumstances surrounding him to tolerate what he abhorred.

The train containing the special ammunition telegraphed for by General McClellan, while the battle of Antietam was pending, was ready at the Washington Arsenal at 1 a. m., of September 18, 1862. Why it did not reach the Northern Central Railway at Baltimore until after 7 o'clock that morning has always been more or less of a mystery.

The train consisted of an engine, tender and four Baltimore and Ohio cars, in the custody of Lieutenant Bradford, of the Ordnance Department. It left Baltimore over the Northern Central Railway, at 7:27 a. m., and moving under the personal supervision of Joseph N. DuBarry, the General Superintendent of that road, reached Bridgeport and was delivered to the Cumberland Valley Railroad at 10:20 a. m. The run, 84 miles, was made in two hours and fifty-three minutes, or an average of one mile in two minutes and three and four-sevenths seconds, or an equivalent of nearly thirty miles per hour.

The train was detained at Bridgeport twenty-four minutes, taking on an additional car of ammunition, which had been loaded at Harrisburg from the Pennsylvania State Arsenal, and in cooling off the journal boxes of the four cars. Leaving Bridgeport at 10:44 a. m., it arrived at Chambersburg at 12 m., and at Hagerstown at 12:42 p. m., making the run over the Cumberland Valley Railroad, a distance of seventy-four miles, in one hour and fifty-eight minutes, or an average of one mile in one minute thirty and six-seventh seconds, an equivalent of over thirty-seven miles an hour. The running time was faster than this, for ten minutes were lost at each, Newville and Chambersburg, in cooling off the boxes; deducting the stops, the speed of the train reached forty-five miles per hour. Such running was never experienced on the Cumberland Valley Railroad before, and has not been equaled since. When the train entered Hagerstown all the journal boxes on the four Baltimore and Ohio cars were ablaze; of this fact I was an eye witness.

The actual running time from Baltimore to Hagerstown, a distance of 158 miles, was four hours and thirty-one minutes, or thirty-six and nine-tenth miles per hour. Perhaps there is not another instance in the history of the world where ammunition has been moved such a distance with so much rapidity, and in the face of smoking and blazing journal boxes on the vehicles carrying it.

Had this ammunition, which was ready at the Washington Arsenal, at 1 o'clock a. m., been moved at a relative speed to Baltimore that it was moved from Baltimore to Hagerstown, it would have reached destination at 7:20 a. m., on the morning after the battle of Antietam and been of some avail to McClellan that day.

Following are copies of telegrams relative to the movement:

"HEADQUARTERS ARMY OF THE POTOMAC,
September 17, 1862, 1:20 p. m.

"*Major General Halleck, General in Chief, Washington:*

"Please take military possession of the Chambersburg and Hagerstown railroad that our ammunition and supplies may be hurried up without delay. We are in the midst of the greatest battle of the war, perhaps of history. Thus far it looks well, but I have great odds against me. Hurry up all the troops possible; our loss has been terrific, but we have gained much ground. I have thrown the mass of the army on the left flank. Burnsides is now attacking the right, and I hold my small reserve, consisting of Porter's (Fifth) Corps, ready to attack the centre as soon as the flank movements are developed. I hope that God will give us a glorious victory.

[Signed]   "GEO. B. MCCLELLAN,
"*Major General Commanding.*"

The despatch of which the above is a copy I received from an orderly of Gen. McClellan on the road between Boonsboro and Hagerstown, took it into Hagerstown and wired it to Washington via Harrisburg, about 4:30 p. m.

"Headquarters Army of the Potomac,
September 17, 1862.

"*Brigadier General Ripley, Chief of Ordnance, Washington, D. C.:*

"If you can possibly do it, force some twenty-pounder Parrott ammunition through to-night via Hagerstown and Chambersburg, to us, near Sharpsburg, Maryland.

[Signed] "Geo. B. McClellan,
"*Major General Commanding.*"

The despatch of which the above is a copy was received by me at dusk, and wired by me to Harrisburg for Washington at once. It did not, however, reach the latter city until 10 p. m.

"Hagerstown, Md.,
September 17, 1862, 9:30 p. m.

"*Brigadier General Ripley, Washington, D. C.:*

"General McClellan desires that duplicate ammunition be sent, one part to Hagerstown and the other to Frederick—twenty-pounder Parrott, ten-pounder Parrott, twelve-pounder Napoleon and thirty-two pounder Howitzer ammunition, and small arm ammunition except .54, .58, .69 and .57; Sharp's ammunition and pistol ammunition.

"N. B. Sweitzer,
"*Lieutenant Colonel and A. D. C.*"

Sent telegram of which above is a copy at hour

Bull Run to Antietam.

indicated via Harrisburg. Its receipt acknowledged at Washington at 10 p. m.

"WAR DEPARTMENT, WASHINGTON, D. C.,
September, 17, 1862.

"*General McClellan, near Hagerstown, Md.:*

"Telegram received. A special train will soon leave with the twenty-pounder ammunition asked for. It will go in charge of an ordnance officer, and will be in Hagerstown to-morrow morning. Other ammunition will follow to Frederick and Hagerstown as soon as possible.
[Signed] "JAS. W. RIPLEY,
"*Brigadier General, Chief of Ordnance.*"

"WAR DEPARTMENT, WASHINGTON, D. C.,
September 17, 1862.

"*John W. Garrett, Esq., President B. and O. R. R., Baltimore, Md.:*

"We are making up a train, to consist of a locomotive and one baggage car, loaded with ammunition which General McClellan wants in the morning loaded at Hagerstown, if possible. This train must have the right of way on the entire route, and must be run as fast as any express passenger train could be run. It will be ready to start in two or three hours from this time. Can you make the necessary arrangements to push it through via Harrisburg?
[Signed] "P. H. WATSON,
"*Assistant Secretary of War.*"

BALTIMORE, MD., September 17, 1862.

"*Hon. P. H. Watson, Assistant Secretary of War, Washington, D. C.:*

"We make arrangements to forward the number of cars stated, without delay. Will send through Northern Central road, and we at once advise that company to make all necessary preparations to transport to Hagerstown as speedily as possible.

[Signed] "J. W. GARRETT,
"*President.*"

"12 P. M., WAR DEPARTMENT, WASHINGTON,
D. C., September 17, 1862.

"*To the Officers or Any of Them of the Northern Central Railroad, Pennsylvania Central Railroad and Cumberland Valley Railroad at Harrisburg, Pa.:*

"An ammunition train will leave here about 1 o'clock a. m. for Hagerstown via Harrisburg, to be run through at the fastest possible speed so as to reach its destination to-morrow morning early. It must have the right of way throughout, as General McClellan needs the ammunition to be used in the battle to be fought to-morrow. It is expected you will use every possible effort to expedite the passing of this train.

"By order of the President of the United States.

[Signed] "EDWIN M. STANTON,
"*Secretary of War.*"

"WAR DEPARTMENT, 12 p. m.,
WASHINGTON, D. C., September 18, 1862.

"*Hon. Thomas A. Scott, Harrisburg:*

"I have telegraphed to the officers of the Northern Central and of the Cumberland Valley Railroads to expedite a train loaded with ammunition, of which General McClellan is in great need, and for which he telegraphed since 10 o'clock p. m. We start the train in about one hour. If we could have the assurance that you would attend personally to securing the right of way for the train and otherwise expediting its passage, we should have strong hope that it would reach its destination early in the morning—in time for the ammunition to be used in the expected battle to-morrow. At all events we should know that nothing would be left undone within the limits of possibilities to get this ammunition to General McClellan in season.

[Signed] "P. H. WATSON,
"*Assistant Secretary of War.*"

"HARRISBURG, PA., Sept. 18, 1862, 1:40 a. m.

"*P. H. Watson, Assistant Secretary of War, Washington, D. C.:*

"I will see the officers in person. No delay shall occur that it is possible to avoid. Can you give me an idea of the number of cars in train, so that suitable power can be ready to move it? Answer immediately.

[Signed] "THOMAS A. SCOTT."

"WASHINGTON, September 18, 1862.
"*Hon. Thomas A. Scott, Harrisburg, Pa.:*
  "The train contains four cars.
  [Signed] "P. H. WATSON,
    "*Assistant Secretary of War.*"

"HARRISBURG, PA., September 18, 1862, 2 a. m.
"*Hon. E. M. Stanton, Secretary of War, Washington, D. C.:*
  "No efforts shall be spared to expedite movements of train. I have already advised officers of all the roads to push it through with preference over all other trains.
  [Signed] "THOMAS A. SCOTT."

"HARRISBURG, PA., September 18, 1862, 8 a. m.
"*Hon. E. M. Stanton, Secretary of War, Washington, D. C.:*
  "The extra ammunition train had not reached Baltimore at 7 o'clock. Is it coming? We have about six car loads of six-pounder artillery, and some musket ammunition, which I am now loading up, and will forward it up the valley if the other cannot reach here. We had arrangements perfected through to move the train forty miles per hour.
  [Signed] "THOMAS A. SCOTT."

"HARRISBURG, PA., September 18, 1862.
"*E. M. Stanton, Secretary of War, Washington, D. C.:*
  "The ammunition train for General McClellan was delivered to the Northern Central Railroad, at

Baltimore, at 7:27 this a. m., and was delivered to the Cumberland Valley Railroad at 10:20 a. m.; eighty-four miles—two hours and fifty-three minutes. It will be put through at the same speed to Hagerstown.

[Signed]   "J. N. Du Barry,
          "*Superintendent.*"

"HARRISBURG, PA., September 18, 1862, 10 a. m.
"*E. M. Stanton, Secretary of War, Washington, D. C.:*

"Hagerstown reports no firing up to 9 o'clock. A rumor is prevalent that McClellan granted armistice to bury dead. Your ammunition train left Baltimore 7:30 and will be put through quick. Governor and staff have gone to Hagerstown to expedite movement of Pennsylvania forces to battle field. Surgeon Smith also gone with forty surgeons.

[Signed]   "THOMAS A. SCOTT."

"WAR DEPARTMENT, WASHINGTON, D. C.
    September 18, 1862, 10 a. m.

"*Major General G. B. McClellan, Commanding Headquarters Army of Potomac, near Sharpsburg, Md.:*

"Your telegram to General Ripley, saying, 'If you can possibly do it force some twenty-pounder Parrott ammunition through to-night, via Hagerstown and Chambersburg, to us near Sharpsburg, Md.,' was received between 10 and 11 o'clock last night, and 2,500 rounds of this ammunition was ordered with the least practicable delay from the arsenal, and arrangements made to run it through on all the roads at express passenger speed. It is now near Harrisburg, Pa., and will reach Hagerstown by noon to-day.

 [Signed]   "P. H. WATSON,
    "*Assistant Secretary of War.*"

   "WASHINGTON, D. C., September 18, 1862.
"*Major General George B. McClellan, near Hagerstown, Md.:*

"Four hundred and fourteen wagon loads of field and small-arm ammunition have been sent to Frederick for your army since Saturday last. Besides this, the duplicate supplies to be sent to Frederick and Hagerstown are being pushed forward with all possible despatch. A special train, containing 2,500 rounds of twenty-pounder ammunition, left last night for Hagerstown in charge of Lieutenant Bradford, Ordnance Department.

 [Signed]   "JAS. W. RIPLEY,
   "*Brigadier General, Chief of Ordnance.*"

     "HARRISBURG, PA.,
   September 18, 1862, 2:30 p. m.
"*Hon. E. M. Stanton, Sec. of War, Washington, D. C.:*

"Ammunition has been delivered at Hagerstown. Stock in this arsenal has gone up by train this p. m. The Governor ordered more ammunition and some arms last night. They are needed. Will they be sent? Chief of Ordnance telegraphs Governor that he refers it to you. Please answer.

 [Signed]   "THOMAS A. SCOTT,
      "*Aid-de-Camp.*"

VI.

A TRIP FROM FREDERICK CITY TO CHAMBERSBURG, AND A VIEW OF THE LATTER'S DESOLATION.

THE burning of Chambersburg, on Saturday, July 30, 1864, by the command of the Confederate General McCausland, composed of his own brigade of mounted infantry, and a brigade of cavalry 3,000 strong, under General Bradley T. Johnson, must ever remain the most wanton, brutal act of all savage acts that here and there blot the fair pages of the nineteenth century's history.

Even at this day, after a quarter of a century has elapsed, I cannot allow my mind to rest upon it without being overcome by a wave of indignation and of horror at the act itself, and a loathing for its author.

The apology, always given without a blush of shame, has been that it was an act of justifiable retaliation prompted by Hunter's deeds in the Shenandoah Valley, but the dwellings that Hunter burned were only those that sheltered and concealed assassins who laid in wait and fired from ambush, while Chambersburg, unfortified, ungarrisoned, had committed no graver offense than that of being true to the Government, and of sending her sons to manly warfare in the open field.

If it was retaliation why was it that, like the demands of that notorious Mexican bandit, Cortinas, a demand for a moneyed ransom preceded the burning? Retaliation forsooth! Jubal Early, thwarted in his designs on Baltimore and Washington, planned and ordered the burning from motives in which plunder, hatred and revenge did not play an inconsequent part.

After General Lew Wallace's hurriedly-gathered and undisciplined command was defeated on the Monocacy by Early, I was making observations on the Potomac, from whence, on the 29th of July, a telegram from Governor Curtin called me into Frederick City. There I was instructed by the Governor, through the medium of the telegraph, that, as the enemy were threatening a raid on Pennsylvania, I should return at once to the border to observe movements and report to him.

Frederick City was at the time in a ferment of excitement over the probability of its being again visited by Early, and, in consequence, it was with extreme difficulty that I could obtain a conveyance to carry me on my way. However, after a number of attempts, I succeeded in employing a man, who, tempted by a ten-dollar bill, agreed to drive me to Emmitsburg, a distance of about twenty-three miles.

As we drove along the road my driver soon began to show signs of nervousness, which were in no sense lessened by the tales of refugees fleeing towards Frederick and from before a supposed foe. At three o'clock in the afternoon, and when ten miles out, the driver's nervousness had degenerated into absolute fear, and stopping the horse he deliberately, and without the least ceremony, threw me out of the buggy on to the roadside, and then drove back over the road we had just come as if all the hates and furies were on his trail. Although put out mentally, as well as bodily, I was thankful for that ten miles' ride, even if it had been at the expense of one dollar per mile, and of a sudden introduction to Mother Earth.

The prospect before me was not the most encouraging, but with youth and health, a love of adventure and a desire to be of service to my country, I took up with some complacency the long and solitary march that laid before me. My every sense was keenly alive and acutely exercised, for I momentarily expected to see the enemy approaching. At the few farm houses I entered to obtain information I was assured, with marked positiveness, that the enemy was only two miles in my advance, and as I continued trudging along every now and then sounds of horses' hoofs on the road would drive me to the cover of fence corners or bushes, only to discover that the supposed foe was nothing more than frightened owners hurrying their horses to a place of safety. Neither the darkness of the night nor the discomforts of a heavy shower deterred my march, and towards midnight I was passing over the ground where a year before the heroic Meade, backed by the grand old Army of the Potomac, had driven off of Pennsylvania soil General Lee and his splendid Army of Northern Virginia. The very ground seemed suggestive to me of strength, and I entered the now historic town of Gettysburg, buoyed up with hope and patriotism, only to find the same alarm existing that had existed at Frederick and along the road I had just traveled. Knowing the necessity for a little rest I threw myself upon the floor of a lawyer's office and took a two hours' nap. Awakening refreshed, and, making preparations for a continued walk, I was greatly relieved by a patriotic citizen volunteering to drive me towards the

Frederick City to Chambersburg.   87

mountains, and in the direction of Chambersburg. A drive of some miles put me well on my way when, after bidding my kind friend good bye, I resumed my lonely march. As I passed down the mountains, the lurid flames shooting far up into the heavens, and the clouds of dense smoke flying over the beautiful Cumberland Valley, told me only too plainly that a great calamity had fallen upon the people of Chambersburg. The story of its nature and extent was borne to my ears by horror-stricken victims before I reached the town.

The afternoon's sun was advancing as I entered the town limits. The vandal's work had been done, and the vandal flown, but, oh! such distress, such desolation may God never again present to my sight. As I viewed the scene I grew heart-sick, and tears unbidden came as the once happy homes were unfolded as smouldering ruins, and their owners as wanderers with no possessions but what they bore upon their persons. People were wandering listlessly among the ruins without permitting a murmur to break upon the ear. This quietness was not, however, a quietness produced by the agony of despair, for all seemed to breathe the prayer of thankfulness that the family circle was complete.

The scene was beyond the power of pen or the

vividness of the imagination—indescribable. None but a fiend, or General Early, could have witnessed it unmoved. It seems horrible to even contemplate such complete ruin befalling a town inhabited by a God-loving people. Picture to yourself a community in full health and prosperity awakening on a bright July morning and sitting around the family boards to partake, in thankfulness, of its morning meal, and as its members talked over their plans for the day, to be suddenly and ruthlessly torn from their tables, to have their houses fired over their heads, themselves driven out on to the highways and byways homeless, almost penniless, fugitives; and as they hurriedly passed over familiar streets, seeking for personal safety, their lives imperiled at every step by flying embers and falling walls, their ears deafened by the fierce, crackling flames, their throats filled with suffocating smoke and their flesh scorched by the merciless heat. If you can imagine the horrors and miseries of such a situation you can then form a faint idea of the surroundings of the Chambersburg people that day. And yet amidst all this, and while standing surrounded by the blackened ruins of their former beautiful town, these people with an exalted moral heroism, the outcome of the teachings of Calvin and of Luther, were talking of issuing a circular to the Union commanders in the field imploring them to respect private property, to protect the women and children, and not to visit upon any Southern community such sufferings as theirs. Is it a matter of wonder that with such Christian charity at such a time that the community so suffering should have arisen from its ashes, as it has, like a new Phœnix, better, more beautiful, more prosperous than before, and that the author of its woes still lingers on the stage of life an exile in his native land?

VII.

THE RAILROAD IN WAR TIMES.

THERE is inherent in the American character a prejudice against corporations, which, at intervals, displays itself in the shape of bitter complaints or noisy clamors. Whenever the interests of the corporation conflict with those of an individual or a class, these displays are sure to occur. On frequent occasions of their occurrence they are accompanied by very pronounced intemperance of language, and with a total disregard of the merits of the question at issue.

The reasons for this manifest injustice are to be found in the fact that the prejudice is but a natural outgrowth of a democratic form of government, and emanates from the innate spirit of opposition of the people forming such a government to any idea which is suggestive of centralized power.

The masses of the people cannot guard with a too jealous strictness their rights as well against encroachments of corporate wealth as against the unhealthy ambitions of partisan leaders. At the same time

they should not forget that corporate wealth gives
the impetus to all kinds of business which insures
that development to a country that the individual
has not the power to produce, and that renders possible the largest meed to follow individual activity,
out of which always emerges enlarged fields of individual independence. Nor must they forget that the
corporation is entitled to the same measure of justice
they demand for themselves.

During the war of the rebellion the corporations
were invaluable factors in maintaining the inviolability of the Union. The patriotic sentiments and
movements of the people were ably supplemented by
the patriotic endeavors of the corporations. It goes
without saying that the unstinted assistance given
by the financial and carrying corporations to the
Government in the hour of its trials made possible
that rehabilitation of the Republic which has enabled
it to spread its beneficent influence throughout the
world, and to rapidly advance the development and
prosperity of its citizens.

Volumes could be written on the greatness and
variety of the service performed on behalf of the
Government by the railroad companies and by the
railroad branch of the army transportation, and of
the ceaseless work of such able and patriotic railroad

officials as Thomas A. Scott, J. Donald Cameron, Samuel M. Felton, J. N. DuBarry, J. H. Devereaux and others, but the scope of this work will not permit of my trenching on the grounds that should be possessed by some able and well-equipped historical writer. My object in touching upon the subject at all is to attract attention to it, and to make record of a long since forgotten act of the great Pennsylvania Railroad Company that never received the credit to which it was entitled. In July, 1862, when the disaster to the Army of the Potomac made urgent the demand for more men and money, the Board of Directors of the Pennsylvania Railroad Company, at their meeting held July 23, 1862, passed the following preambles and resolution:

WHEREAS, It is officially declared by the Executive of the State of Pennsylvania, that a public emergency demands the prompt co-operation and financial aid of the people of the State to enable the Government to ensure just and efficient security to the citizens of this Commonwealth against the various contingencies incident to the prevailing civil war; and

WHEREAS, The interests of this Company, and the protection of its property as well as that of the citizens of Pennsylvania, are directly involved in the perfect maintenance of such public security; therefore be it

Resolved, That the President of the Pennsylvania Railroad Company be and he is hereby authorized to advance from time to time, as the same may be needed, to the Executive of the State of Pennsylvania, or such agents as may be organized by him for the purpose of disbursing the Bounty Fund, contributed by the people of Pennsylvania, the sum of fifty thousand dollars, to be applied to the payment of bounty to soldiers, enlisting in the service of the Government.

Governor Curtin not having any authority, as Governor, to accept and disburse this money, under date of October 4, 1862, wrote a letter to the Board stating that he must decline receiving the donations as Governor, as the money could not be disbursed through any official channel and no legal restraint could be thrown over the faithful appropriation of it, and suggesting that the resolution be changed so as to appropriate the money to the use of Volunteers, in Pennsylvania, then in the service, in such manner as would promote their efficiency and comfort, and offered a hearty co-operation in whatever was proposed in that respect.

In reply to this communication it was recommended by the Board that the donation be used as part of a fund for the establishment of a Soldier's Home at or near Harrisburg, or as an annuity for the same to provide for the comfort of disabled volunteers from our Commonwealth.

Governor Curtin, accepting this recommendation, sent a special message to the Legislature early in 1863, urgently advising the acceptance of the gift and its appropriation in the direction indicated, but the Legislature took no action, and the gift remained unaccepted, although not lost sight of by the Governor. Between the adjournment of the Legislature of 1863 and the convening of that of 1864 he had several conferences with the officers of the company, and by their advice and consent he again, in 1864, sent a message to the Legislature urging the acceptance of the money and its application to the fostering, as the children of the Commonwealth, the poor orphans of Pennsylvania soldiers who had already given up, or might thereafter give up, their lives for the country in the then present crisis. The Legislature acted sluggishly and stintingly, and without adding one cent of additional money for the object, passed after much debate the following act:

"Section 1. Be it enacted, etc., That the Governor of the Commonwealth be and is hereby authorized to accept the sum of $50,000 donated by the Pennsylvania Railroad Company, for the education and maintenance of destitute orphan children of deceased soldiers and sailors, and appropriate the same in such manner as he may deem best calculated to accomplish the object designed by said donation; the accounts of said disbursements to be settled in the usual manner by the Auditor General and the Governor, and make report of the same to the next Legislature."

Approving the act as soon as it reached him, Governor Curtin at once appointed the Hon. Thomas H. Burrowes Superintendent of Soldiers' Orphans' Schools, and thus by the broad generosity of the Pennsylvania Railroad Company launched that great charity which is one of the brightest glories of the Quaker Commonwealth. As these facts prove that Republics are not ungrateful, they also give evidence that corporations are possessed of souls.

VIII.

U. S. MILITARY TELEGRAPH CORPS.

To the memory of my comrades who fell during the civil war, sacrifices to patriotic duty, well performed, this paper is lovingly dedicated by the author.

THE golden dream of empire, which had haunted the waking and sleeping moments of the cultivated aristocratic ruling class of the Gulf States, and of the land barons of South Carolina and Georgia, aided and abetted by impracticable legislation and fanatical expressions of latitudinarian doctrines of government by agitators throughout the Northern States, had at last brought about that most deplorable of all conflicts—civil war. It was a serious hour for the principles of self-government by the people as represented by the Constitution of the great American Republic.

Sumter had been fired upon, and the emblem of our nationality was lowered at the demand of revolting citizens.

In this crisis, President Lincoln called upon the

U. S. Military Telegraph Corps.

various States for 75,000 men to restore the authority of the National Government.

In response to that call, the men, who in the preceding election had voted in the North for Lincoln, for Breckenridge, for Douglas and for Bell, with a fair number of Union-loving men from the South, rushed forward, as with a common impulse, shoulder to shoulder, with a patriotic impetus inborn of love for and devotion to country.

I can yet hear the swish of the waves of patriotism as they broke upon the shores of rebellion.

No person rushed with more patriotic fervor to the field of Mars than did the boys of the telegraph. It was my fortune to be made manager of the military telegraph office in the War Department early in the struggle, and it is, therefore, with confidence I speak of the organization and efficiency of the Military Telegraph Corps of the United States Army.

On the 27th of April, 1861, on the order of Simon Cameron, then Secretary of War, David Strouse, Homer Bates, Samuel Brown and Richard O'Brien, four of the best and most reliable operators on the Pennsylvania Railroad Company's telegraph line, arrived in Washington and formed, under Thomas A. Scott, of Philadelphia, the germ out of which grew the best disciplined, the most wonderfully accurate, reliable and intelligent army telegraph corps ever known to the world. The quartette was rapidly followed by others, until, throughout the length and breadth of the army, over twelve hundred young men enrolled themselves in the corps, and rendered such services as had never before been performed for any Government. Their ages ranged from sixteen to twenty-two years—boys in years, boys in stature, but giants in loyalty, and giants in the amount of work they performed for their country.

A better-natured, more intelligent-looking or harder-working band of young men did not exist in the army. They were ready and willing to go anywhere at a moment's notice, and, if necessary, to work day and night without rest uncomplainingly. Oft times they were sent where the sky was the only protecting roof over their heads, a tree stump their only office, and the ground their downy couch. Provisioned with a handful of hard bread, a canteen of water, pipe, tobacco-pouch and matches, they would open and work an office at the picket line in order to keep the commanding general in instantaneous communication with his most advanced forces, or to herald the first approach of the enemy. When retreat became necessary it was their place to remain behind and to announce that the rear guard had passed the danger line between it and the pursuing foe.

All the movements of the army, all the confidence of the commanders were entrusted to these boys, and yet not one was ever known to betray that knowledge and confidence in the most remote degree.

The military telegraph eventually assumed, under General Eckert, colossal proportions, its ramifications extending to every portion of the Union where a Union soldier could be found. Its delicate, yet potent, power was felt and appreciated by every department of the Government. The system, as perfected, was elaborate and complete in all its details. The boys constructed and operated during the war, within the lines of the army, 15,389 miles of telegraph, and transmitted over 6,000,000 military telegrams. Of the latter a large proportion were in the secret cipher of the Government, the keys of which were solely in the possession of the operators.

The boys didn't plan campaigns or fight battles, but amidst the fiercest roar of conflict they were to be found coolly advising the commanding general of the battle's progress.

When the army, in all its grand divisions, was in motion they were to be found in the advance, in the rear, on right, left and center—wherever duty was to be performed; and when the army was in repose a thousand general officers had them at their elbows.

The corps was the very nerves of the army during the war, and was so considered by all those that came in contact with it, and yet it was not, and has not been, recognized as an integral part of that army.

Its services were great; its sacrifices many. Beginning at Yorktown, where poor Lathrop was murdered by one of Magruder's buried torpedoes, from East to West and North to South, as our grand armies marched and fought, until Rebellion's knell was sounded at Appomattox, almost every field, almost every march numbered one of the telegraph boys among the fallen.

A hundred nameless graves throughout the battlefields of the Union attest their devotion unto death to the sublime cause in which they were engaged, and yet the Government they loved and labored for never as much as thanked them for their services. It is a sad reflection when old memories come back, that of the twelve hundred boys composing that corps there are not three hundred left. Where are the remainder? Those that did not lay down their lives in action succumbed shortly after the war from wounds, and from the effects of exposures and imprisonments.

Here let me say of the dead: Not a funeral note was sounded as they passed into the earth; not a flower is cast upon their mounds as Memorial Day comes around.

And of the survivors: Not a door swings upon its hinges to welcome them into any of the various organizations of the loyal men who fought the battles of the Union.

A few of the officers were commissioned, and, in consequence, are borne upon the rolls of honor, but the rank and file, who performed the principal duties, although obliged to take an oath of allegiance and of secrecy, not being technically sworn into the service, were disbanded without a word of thanks or a scrap of paper showing that they had honorably discharged their trying duties.

Secretary of War Stanton said, in one of his reports to Congress: "The military telegraph has been of inestimable value to the service, and no corps has surpassed it."

Since the war Congress has been appealed to to right the wrongs and enroll the corps, but, notwithstanding Grant, McClellan, Hancock, Sherman, Sheridan, Burnsides, Warren, Rosecranz, Sanborn,

Porter, Smith and others have urged that the services of the corps were invaluable, and its members shamefully treated; and General Logan, J. Donald Cameron and General Hawley exerted their utmost endeavors, from their seats in the United States Senate, to have justice done, the wrong remains unrighted.

'Twas an hour fraught with gloom, when the maddened bullet, speeding from the murderer's weapon, laid low the head of that mighty chieftain, who was the one, had life been spared him, that would have seen justice done the corps. But the corps, like humanity in general, suffered when Abraham Lincoln died.

It was through my connection with the corps that I became acquainted with Mr. Lincoln, and it is for that reason I have grouped a glimpse of him with a glimpse of it.

IX.

ABRAHAM LINCOLN.

THE multitude of sketches that have been written on the life, character and public services of Abraham Lincoln make me hesitate in speaking of the impressions of him that were left on my mind by daily contact with him during the first year of his administration of the Presidency. This hesitation is rather increased than diminished when I consider that his fulsome eulogists, under the garb of confidential friends, have so surrounded his memory with a halo of deity that to speak of him as I saw him may be looked upon as a misrepresentation. The tragedy of his death, and the tight hold he had upon the popular heart at that time created the opportunity for opening the flood-gates of flattery, which, to a great extent, have obscured the true character of the man.

I first saw him in Harrisburg, on an evening in February, 1861, as he emerged from the side door of the Jones House, in the judicious act of flanking any hostile movement that might be developed by the threatening attitude of Baltimore as he proceeded to Washington and his fate. At that time, although conceding to him honesty of intention, I did not accept him as an oracle. My political education had been in the strict construction school, and I had only then returned from South Carolina to place myself on the side of the Union. Knowing the earnestness and intensity of the feeling in the South I looked upon his speeches from the text of "nobody hurt" as belittling the gravity of the situation. Towards the close of April, 1861, however, I was called to Washington as military telegrapher in the Departpartment of War, and in that capacity came in contact with Mr. Lincoln many times daily, and often late at nights. He was always on terms of easy familiarity with the operators, and it was through that familiarity that my acquaintance with him was formed.

I soon saw a man before me with a kind heart and charitable disposition, who had a duty to perform that he intended performing with a conscientious exactitude. In the many telegrams he indited or dictated, and in the conversations he had with Secretary of State Seward, who almost invariably accompanied him to the war telegraph office, he displayed a wonderful knowledge of the country, its resources and requirements, as well as an intuition of the needs and wants of the people.

He was entirely unselfish, and in his exalted position did not seen to think of himself for himself. The great cause of perpetuating the Government entrusted to his care seemed to absorb his whole time and thought. When he acted it was from a sense of duty, and whatever the effect such action might have upon himself I don't think influenced him pro or con.

There was nothing ornamental in or about him, and to depict him in the ornamental light is to detract from his true greatness, which consisted of his being a true representative of a great people and a great principle of government.

Mr. Lincoln's shining characteristic was his extreme simplicity. He thoroughly recognized the true import of his position to be the serving of the people, and he tried to so conduct the administration of affairs that whoever looked upon him in the presidential chair should see reflected the power, the intelligence, the charity, the greatness of a great nation. His acts were all studied in the school of duty, and were, to the extent of his information, the expressions of the national will. This was nowhere more notable than in his issuance of the Emancipation Proclamation. To make him a god of freedom on account of his promulgating that paper which released the country from the curse of slavery is to give him attributes he never claimed, and to imply motives he would have spurned.

The Emancipitation Proclamation was not issued solely in the cause of freedom, or solely to liberate the slaves, for Mr. Lincoln and the political party which had elevated him to the presidential office were committed to the strange doctrine that although slavery was an evil not to be extended yet it was to be tolerated and protected because of its existence. He announced most earnestly in his inaugural address that he had no purpose to interfere, directly or indirectly, with the institution of slavery in the States where it existed. That he did not depart from that policy until he was obliged to do so by the stern necessities of war and the readiness of the people for such departure, is a matter of historical fact. It is true he entertained emancipation views, but they were based upon emancipation by compensation, attended by colonization that was to be reached through independent State action. When General John Cochrane, of New York, in the fall of 1861, suggested and advocated the arming of the slaves, and Simon Cameron pressed for the same object in Cabinet councils, both knowing that it was a practical emancipation measure, and that the slave, by its adoption, would become his own emancipator, Mr. Lincoln did not second them in their efforts because he did not think it the will of the people.

He declared his purpose to be the execution of the laws and the maintaining the union of the States inviolate. But as the war of the rebellion drew on apace, larger and larger in its proportions, and fiercer and fiercer in its animosities, with variable results to the contending parties, the emancipation of the slaves became an absolute military necessity and with that came the Emancipation Proclamation. Its origin and standing rests nowhere else. The slaves were declared free, not because slavery was wrong, but for the same reason that the enemy's horses, cattle, houses, wagons and lands were taken from him,—to cripple him in his resources.

It was duty to the country, not justice to the slave, and Abraham Lincoln claimed no other credit.

He was not a god, and it is unseemly sacrilege to paint him in colors wherein he might be mistaken for such. He was a man with all the attributes that enter into manhood. He had all the tastes, ambitions, affections, longings and passions of other men, but he had them under complete control, so that they might be used for the benefit of common humanity, and not alone for self-gratification.

There was nothing false about him, for while he might curtain his thoughts and intentions as a matter of temporary policy it was not for the purpose of deception, but simply to guard against the plucking of unripe fruit.

It was not into ancestors' graves that Abraham Lincoln dug for the clothes that were to clothe him in the garb of manhood. He studied the laws of his Creator to find the material from which to shape them, and he found it.

Despoiled of his titles, honor and power, and introduced solely as the homely, honest man he was, into that American society that seeks the tracery of a ducal coronet on its escutcheon, and that obtains its principal sustenance from the phosphorescent light emanating from the bones of long buried ancestors, he would have been thrust out as an unwelcome guest.

Whilst he was kind and tolerant to those of different opinions from his, and freely communicated with all those with whom he came in contact, yet he impressed me with being a man who had but one confidant, and that confidant himself.

Before coming to a conclusion, I will narrate some anecdotes of the man that came under my personal observation:

In the fall of 1861 fires in Washington City were of frequent occurrence, without any organized adequate means for rapidly extinguishing them being in existence there. This condition of affairs was a source of so much anxiety to the country at large that no sooner was a Washington fire announced in the newspapers of the principal cities than the mails would teem with patriotic offers to the President, from all sections, for the formation of fire brigades, as a component part of the army, for the protection of the Capital. This was one of the many great annoyances of irrelevant subjects thrust upon the President in those trying times, but he bore it all as part of the responsibilities resting upon him; yet at last he was compelled to rebuke it from sheer lack of time to give it any attention. One night the Washington Infirmary burned down, and, as was customary after such a disaster, the next day brought the President the usual complement of offers for fire engines and firemen. Philadelphia's patriotism, true to its traditions, could not await the slow progress of the mail, but sent forward a committee of citizens to urge upon the President the acceptance of a fully equipped fire brigade for Washington. On their arrival at the White House they were duly ushered into the Executive Chamber and courteously and blandly received by Mr. Lincoln. Eloquently did they urge the cause of their mission, but valuable time was being wasted, and Mr. Lincoln was forced to bring the conference to a close, which he did by interrupting one of the committee in the midst of a grand and to-be-clinching oratorical effort, by gravely saying, and as if he had just awakened to the true import of the visit, "Ah! Yes, gentlemen, but it is a mistake to suppose that I am at the head of the fire department of Washington. I am simply the President of the United States." The quiet irony had its proper effect, and the committee departed.

The personal familiarity of Mr. Lincoln, shown in his intercourse with the war telegraphers already spoken of, cannot be better illustrated than by relating a few personal encounters with him.

September 27, 1861, was an appointed day for humiliation, fasting and prayer, and was generally observed throughout the North. We operators on the military telegraph were extra vigilant at our posts; our boy George was engaged in preparing a 'Daniel's battery" when, shortly after noon, Mr. Lincoln entered the War Department office. Spying George, he accosted him with "Well, sonny, mixing the juices, eh?" Then taking a seat in a large arm-chair and adjusting his spectacles, he became aware that we were very busy. A smile broke over his face as he saluted us with "Gentlemen, this is fast day, and I am pleased to observe that you are working as fast as you can; the proclamation was mine, and that is my interpretation of its bearing upon you." Then, changing the subject, he said, "Now, we will have a little talk with Governor Morton, at Indianapolis. I want to give him a lesson in geography. Bowling Green affair I set him all right upon; now I will tell him something about Muldraugh Hill. Morton is a good fellow, but at times he is the skeeredest man I know of."

It was customary for Mr. Lincoln to make frequent calls at the war telegraph office, either for the purpose of direct telegraphic communication or to obtain what he called news. One day in September, 1861, accompanied by Mr. Seward, he dropped into the office with a pleasant "Good morning; what news?" Responding to the salutation, I replied, "Good news, because none." Whereupon he rejoined, "Ah! my young friend, that rule don't always hold good, for a fisherman don't consider it good luck when he can't get a bite."

On another day, also accompanied by Secretary Seward, he came into the office. They seemed to have escaped from some one who had been boring them, and the President appeared to be greatly relieved as he sank into an arm-chair, saying, "By Jings, Governor, we are here." Mr. Seward turned to him and, in a manner of semi-reproof, said, "Mr. President, where did you learn that inelegant expression?" Without replying, Mr. Lincoln turned to us and said, "Young gentlemen, excuse me for swearing before you; by jings is swearing, for my good old mother taught me that anything that had a *by* before it is swearing. I won't do so any more."

Mr. Lincoln was entirely free from political intolerance, although at times he was compelled to permit its exercise by others. I experienced an application of his broad views. A few days prior to the Pennsylvania election, in October, 1861, I went to the White House and reported to the President that I was going over to Pennsylvania for a few days, and that I would leave the war telegraph office in charge of Mr. Homer Bates, who would keep him as thoroughly advised of passing events as I had been doing. With his peculiarly humorous smile breaking over his face, he said, "All right, my young friend, but before you go tell me if you ain't going over to

Pennsylvania to vote?" I replied affirmatively, adding that it would be my first vote in my native State. Upon his questioning me still further, I told him I was a Democrat in politics, and expected to vote for the ticket of that party. Then, with the remark "Oh, that's all right! Only be sure you vote for the right kind of Democrats," he bade me good-bye.

On the 27th of August, 1861, our pickets beyond Ball's Cross Roads had been driven in and an attack upon our lines was anticipated, the enemy being reported as advancing in force along the railroad. General McClellan was on the Virginia side giving his personal attention to his command. About nine o'clock in the evening Mr. Lincoln, in company with two other gentlemen, came into the office to be "posted." I told the President that General McClellan was on his way from Arlington to Fort Cochrane, that our picket's still held Ball's and Bailey's Cross Roads, and that no firing had been heard since sunset. The President then inquired if any firing had been heard *before* sunset, and upon my replying there had been none reported, laughingly said, "That puts me in mind of a party who, in speaking of a freak of nature, described it as a child who was black from the hips down, and, upon being asked the color from the hips up, replied *black*, as a matter of course."

I could go on indefinitely relating such anecdotes, but I refrain, and will conclude by saying:

Abraham Lincoln will live in the correct history of his times as one who was unflinching in his devotion to duty, unswerving in his fidelity to a great cause; one whose every breath poured forth the purest sentiments of patriotism; and as one who tried to live a manly life within the bounds of his comprehension of manhood's aims and duties.

www.ingramcontent.com/pod-product-compliance
Lightning Source LLC
Chambersburg PA
CBHW020143170426
43199CB00010B/870